Storytellers

Storytellers

The Image of The Two-Year College in American Fiction and in Women's Journals

by
Nancy LaPaglia

LEPS Press, Northern Illinois University
DeKalb, Illinois 60115

© by LEPS Press
All rights reserved. Published 1994
Printed in the United States of America

Managing Editor: Caryn Rudy
Cover Illustration: Katrina Elisa Davis-Salazar

Distributed by LEPS Press

Library of Congress Catalog-in-Publication Data

LaPaglia, Nancy.
　Storytellers : the image of the two-year college in
American fiction and in women's journals / by Nancy
LaPaglia.
　　　　　p.　　　　　cm.
　Includes bibliographical references.
　ISBN 1-879528-07-X
　1. Junior colleges—United States. 2. Community col-
leges—United States. 3. College stories, American. 4. Lit-
erature—United States—Women authors. 5. Scholarly
periodicals—United States. 6. Working class (Education)—
Higher—United States. 7. Women—Education (Higher)—
United States. I. Title.
LB2326.7L37　　　1993　　　　　　　　　93-37645
378.1'543'0973—dc20　　　　　　　　　　CIP

Table of Contents

Preface vii

Acknowledgements ix

Introduction: Working-Class Academics xi

1. Dissonant Images 1

2. The Single-Mention List 23

3. Two-Year College Students in Fiction 31

4. Student Journals 57

5. Two-Year College Faculty in Fiction 89

6. Faculty Journals 105

7. Writing The Journals 131

8. Conclusion 145

Sources Consulted 161

Index 171

Preface

This book is a series of stories. I tell two stories of my own, the first of which may reveal the assumptions and biases I bring to the study of the two-year college. My second story explains how I got started on this particular project. For more stories, I looked at all of the American fiction I could find that includes, however peripherally, two-year college characters. Some of these works of the imagination are considered "serious" literature, and some come from popular culture or mass market entertainment.

The fictional characters supposedly reflect the lives of actual two-year college inhabitants. The stereotypical student turned out to be a white, working-class woman of "non-traditional" age. Therefore, I asked two dozen women from across the country who actually live in the circumstances that the writers fictionalize to tell their own stories, using the format of journals kept specifically for my use. Over a dozen two-year college teachers—all experienced women faculty—wrote journals also, so that I might have stories that reflect on the two-year college and its students from yet another viewpoint.

The perspectives are contradictory. After a thematic analysis of the data, it became clear that there is a dissonance between fiction's image of the two-year college (and the view of our culture at large, since that is what fiction mirrors) and the image held by these women themselves. I wished to explore that dissonance. I knew from many years of experience that large numbers of people were being left out of the general view. Further, our society's professional storytellers usually ignore two-year college people altogether, making them almost invisible in importance, perhaps even to themselves.

In this study, I attempt to present a narrative collage of two kinds of data—the stories of fiction writers and the autobiographies of amateur "insiders," in order to describe the picture they hold in their minds as clearly as I can. I tried to figure out some things we take for granted—challenging the "official" depiction by bringing previously unheard groups of people into the story. Society's negative definition and "invisibilization" of many millions of people does them unwarranted harm. We need to hear the rich and moving stories of these women, so that two-year college inhabitants can take part in defining their own experience.

Acknowledgements

Without the enthusiastic support and encouragement of Sherman Stanage, Professor of Philosophy at Northern Illinois University, and of Stephen Slusarski, my husband, this study would not have been finished. Phyllis Cunningham, Joan Kerber, and Betty Holman helped me well beyond anything required by their connection to my work. Glenn Smith, Maurice McNeil, Caryn Rudy, Corinne Allen McArdle and Beverly Tinsley were there when I needed them.

Scores of people took the time to send me leads to fictional characters. Valued friends, Alice and Michael Powell in Oregon and Peter and Nancy Rabinowitz in upstate New York, gave me a home during the week I spent in each state. The Community College Cohort, of which Joan and Maurice are members, formed a true cohort in the original sense: A company of persons united in the defense of a common cause. The life of every writer might be made more bearable by such a group.

And, lastly, it must be clear that I could never have accomplished this work at all without my thirty-seven co-writers, the women who wrote journals so that a stranger from Chicago could complete her book.

Introduction: Working-Class Academics

It's hard to be politically conscious and upwardly mobile at
the same time.[1]

Much as in Edie's dilemma, it is hard to come from
the working class (and remain politically conscious
of it), and be an academic (with its implication of upward
mobility). For some of us, it means not really belonging to
either culture. To choose one over the other might also mean
opting for the selective sight that ambition confers on the
upwardly mobile, or being narrowed by the constraints imposed on working class women.

I like academics as a group. They are smart, funny
(witty), reasonable, and they usually talk rather than hit
people. But I still think of them as "them," although I have
graduate degrees and have been on a college faculty for

---

[1] Jane Wagner's line for Lily Tomlin's Edie, a 1970s radical feminist; Jane
Wagner, *The Search for Signs of Intelligent Life in the Universe* (New York: Harper
& Row, 1986), 193.

decades. For one thing, I am not comfortable with middle-class gentility, which I often read negatively as "passionless" or "distanced."

Are academics maybe too clever? Their very reasonable-ness can strike me as hair-splitting; *I* am more likely to jump to immediate conclusions. Articulate? That can become "wordy" or "precious," although I myself talk a great deal. I was raised working class, and I think what I am describing is suspicion generated by class difference.

I grew up in an ethnic factory neighborhood, and my father was an ironworker (when he wasn't a sort of itinerant gambler). My mother was the designated caretaker of the sick and elderly in an extended family. Her life served as a cautionary tale for me; it functioned as a clear example of what I did not want to be. While one or two relatives gave lip service to the value of an education, I was the first person in my family to graduate from high school.

When I think of the impact of this background on my life and work, I picture someone with one foot in the working class and one foot on a ladder going up, unwilling to commit to a single, more stable stance. To do so would mean betrayal and treachery in some nebulous way. My awkward posture is made easier, if not more graceful, by the fact that although I have a proper academic rank (professor), degree (doctorate) and discipline (the humanities), I am on the faculty of a community college, which is not seen as "really" academic by most who are affiliated with four-year schools. Therefore, I usually don't feel like an outsider with my community college colleagues, though interacting with a few of particu-larly WASPish bent can still make me uncomfortable. Most often, I identify strongly with my working-class students, so that when I finally got around to writing a doctoral disserta-tion, I chose to write about them (and thus about myself).

I grew up feeling an outsider in my own immigrant neighborhood, located in an old industrial suburb of Chicago that was and is famous for gangsters and racism. (My grandmother never criticized Al Capone, because "he always took good care of his mother," who lived in a nearby bungalow. Martin Luther King later threatened to march in this town, which served as a symbol of American racism in the North.) Except for the few Greek families, who maintained their language and customs with ferocity, there was a great emphasis among the various eastern and southern European nationalities on becoming "an American," a determination usually unspoken but nonetheless clear. Becoming an American meant speaking only English and getting a good steady factory job if male, or a temporary clerical job until marriage if female. An occasional very bright boy whose father had moved up to a white-collar job could think about college and a better-paid profession. Boys from mob-connected families had another path they could take. Bright girls who wanted to fit in "knew their place." They were expected to dampen any impulse to excel intellectually and to follow the pattern of their mothers.

In my working class milieu I was partly an insider—I had friends, did well in school, I was even a leader at times in sports and student organizations. However, I had inappropriate interests in things like books (tried to read my way through the public library) and socio-political reform (was called things like "n....lover," and I still can't write or say the word). I was an outsider also because my mother was Jewish, the eastern Europeans in the area were strongly anti-Semitic, and simple childhood quarrels could end with someone screaming, "You killed Jesus!" I never felt that I actually did kill Jesus, but I learned that my own neighborhood held no happy future for me, and that I needed a way out.

I knew that college was a possible escape from my mother's life and the narrow biases of the neighborhood. I am not sure why, since I knew no one who was an academic, and knew about college only from reading. I had read a book by Bertrand Russell called *The Conquest of Happiness*, a brief guide he wrote in 1930 for ordinary readers, and I retained a strong memory of a chapter that declared, "If you are unhappy, maybe you're in the wrong place."[2] I was looking for a place where smart girls were accepted. (Skimming through this book recently, I was unable to find even a paragraph, much less a chapter, on the topic of being in the wrong place, but I must have gotten the message somehow, perhaps out of my own psyche as I read it.)

I went to the local junior college my first year, until I found the audacity, the tuition scholarship and the room-and-board money to leave for the University of Illinois at Urbana-Champaign. That freshman year at a two-year college prepared me well academically for downstate and did not constitute stepping off the flat earth. I could make the break in cultures more gradually.

Before I left for Urbana, I worked as a car hop to earn the money I would need. I liked the uniform (white cowboy boots, abbreviated red shorts, prim Peter Pan-collared blouse), the generous tips, and the hard work that made the time pass faster than the secretarial work I had done earlier at Western Electric. The other employees were not saving for college, however, and I had to work equally hard at not appearing "stuck-up." Admitting to ability or intelligence was a great sin, and indicated that you were "stuck on yourself."

---

[2] Bertrand Russell, *The Conquest of Happiness* (New York: Liveright Publishing, 1930).

One hot Sunday morning, waiting for opening time, we sat around outside with the cooks, reading the newspaper. I asked for the funnies; they were taken. "Well, give me the book section, then." "The *book* section, she wants the BOOOOOK section. La-di-dah." And most nights after our midnight closing, the car hops went to a local bar, where we were supposed to treat each other and friends to drinks. I was never able to make a clear decision about what to do in this situation. I did not want to be an outcast, but I was saving my tips for college. I would go along sometimes, but not frequently. I would drink a little and maybe buy a round, but not always. I was not strong enough or insightful enough to reject that part of working class life completely.

There were good times. *Guys and Dolls* was playing in Chicago, and a friend took me. I loved it, thought the other car hops would as well, and organized an excursion downtown. (This was an early example of the missionary impulse, or more accurately perhaps, sharing impulse, I would later have as a teacher trying to connect cultures and social classes.) I think they liked the musical, but what I remember best are the outfits they wore. They matched those worn by Nathan Detroit's lady-friend, Miss Adelaide, on stage. Tight, lots of draped fabric, heavy make-up and fish-net stockings. Maybe I looked much the same to others in the audience, but I did not think so at the time. I don't remember what I wore, but I was not embarrassed by the group I was with or by my own attire. I already knew I was not a real member of their circle, nor yet of any other.

Just before I left for Urbana, I was "taught a lesson" by the other car hops, so I wouldn't go away thinking I was better than they were. The drive-in was a hang-out for guys who did expensive things to their cars—souped them up, chromed the engines, etc. They would drive in, pop the hood for admirers, and only later order hamburgers. I stayed clear of them pretty much, but when the handsomest, to my mind, asked me to go out with him on my off-night, I agreed. I spent a long time getting ready for the date, and had trouble hours later accepting the fact that I had been stood up.

Still later, I had even more difficulty realizing that the incident was deliberately planned. Perhaps, in their view, it was an appropriate act because they were somehow being stood-up by me. I know that they were angry that I could just quit and walk away, and some of them felt they could not even take time off for a high school prom. (Actually, although I did not realize it at the time, they had the same financial options as I did, but for other reasons made the drive-in and its romantic/sexual entanglements a center of their lives.)

So I went off to the university and never came back home to stay. I never stopped going to college, off and on, despite four children and a full-time job. For many years now, I have felt like a middle-aged Alice in Wonderland, wandering around academe, discovering and trying out new things. Virtually everything has been interesting. I had the great good fortune to find something that I liked to do for a living, and it took me a long time to get over my astonishment that someone was willing to pay me for doing it. This was not "work" as I knew it from my background.

Eventually I became a little more focused on research and wrote my doctoral dissertation on the image of the community college and its inhabitants, a topic that allowed me to straddle social classes, like my stance. Why did it take me so long? I think I am a passionate teacher, for which my early working-class schools offered models. Research, which is the only true currency for most academics, was relatively unknown to me. I chose to do it from time to time. For instance, in the late 1970s and early '80s, I wrote articles on women painters before the nineteenth century. However, when more and better-trained feminist art historians started publishing, I was happy to leave the field to them and use their results and their slides in my classes.

Finally, in the 1990s, there was some knowledge I wanted to produce or discover about another group of women, those affiliated with community colleges. They are considered marginal to academia and in the larger culture, and they are customarily unstudied by others, or by themselves. I had another mission, another part of experience I wished to share.

I became convinced that the demeaning generalizations about community college people come as much from class bias, sexism, and racism as from any actual presence or absence of academic standards. The re-entry women students I studied frequently undergo a transformation that rewards any on the two-year college faculty who care to see it. Not the transformation into physical beauty that our fairy tales and advertising extol for women, but one marked by the joy of learning and accomplished in the face of adversity. The prize won is not a handsome prince, but some control of one's own life. I also studied their teachers, colleagues I admire, who are dedicated people maintaining college standards despite overwork and a society that considers them beneath notice.

Feminism has helped me reconcile the two different worlds of the working class and academia. There is an attempt by many feminists to bridge the gap, and I can see that women face some common problems everywhere. I am allowed to ally myself with women at four-year schools and not feel like a deserter. On their part, there is sometimes, unfortunately, that condescending "apology" made on my behalf. "Don't feel bad that you're only at a community college—some good work can come out of those places." This can still take me by surprise, as I was not feeling bad before I heard them say it.

Slurs of this sort can be found almost everywhere in academia, certainly not just among feminists. The underlying, and sometimes openly spoken, assumption is that anyone who works in such a low-status institution is not interested in even *reading* research, much less producing it.

The somewhat informal, conversational style you are reading here is what I usually insist on using. "Breezy," a dissertation committee member once called it; "flippant" or "too casual," I think she meant. My writing style is part of my unresolved stance. I keep identifying academic writing with jargon and obscurity, although the academic writers I admire, like Wayne Booth and Jill Ker Conway, write with grace and clarity. A lot of evidence contradicts my negative generalizations about traditional academic expression, and I am working on getting past my bias when it is unwarranted.

Despite the inconsistencies of my balancing act, I have a rewarding professional and personal life. When I was young it seemed to me that everything came about almost by accident, "accident" in the way that working-class heroines operate in Bobbie Ann Mason or Joyce Carol Oates stories, though their characters usually have less happy results than mine. Much of my life just sort of happened, I used to feel, and I saw things mostly in the present tense even when I was trying to think ahead. This lack of a sense of agency, of taking credit or being in control, is, I think, partly due to being raised working class and partly to a prevailing pattern of female development. It does not fit well with the values of academic life.

My position between the working class and academia offers the advantage of a kind of double vision, insider/outsider, if I am careful to look in both directions. Recently I listened to a bright University of Chicago student, one who presented herself as a radical feminist, dismiss a largely working class and minority university in her own city because she had "never even *heard* of it!" although it sponsors feminist practices she admires. I should not be too hard on her—she is young and she is typical of a selective elitist vision.

I try not to make the mistake of seeing singly, although constantly recognizing two sides can lead me to be hypersensitive and quarrelsome. What I want to do is remain open to the fact that good things and bad can come from many directions.

Although I recognize that dissimilar domains exist, I want to be everyplace. I am not actually alienated from either sphere—the working class or academia. Maybe I can justify my attempt to be in two places at once, or at least make myself feel better about my awkward posture, by quoting Balzac. "I belong to the party of the opposition which is called life."[3] I am not simply rebelling. I am opposing fixity and trying to have the best of both worlds.

---

[3] Honoré de Balzac, quoted by Albert J. Guerard in the Introduction to Saul Bellow, *The Adventures of Augie March* (Greenwich, CT: Fawcett Publications, 1967), xii.

Chapter 1

Dissonant Images

Something is happening. Norma Jean is going to night
school. She has graduated from her six-week body-building
course and now she is taking an adult-education course in
composition at Paducah Community College. She spends her
evenings outlining paragraphs.

Bobbie Ann Mason, "Shiloh"[1]

These are the thoughts of Leroy Moffitt, Norma Jean's
husband. A former long-distance trucker, he is home
collecting temporary disability, unready to face another job
since he injured his leg in an accident. Norma Jean is strength-
ening mind and body in order to stand up to Leroy and to
Mabel Beasley, her domineering mother.

She is thirty-four, she works at the Rexall cosmetics
counter, and their only child died of sudden infant death

---

[1] Bobbie Ann Mason, "Shiloh," in *Shiloh and Other Stories* (New York:
Harper & Row, 1982), 11.

syndrome seventeen years ago. Her life just sort of happened, but now she gropingly ventures to take some control of it, testing different paths and solutions. She has chosen to stop smoking, and she makes a first attempt at dealing with the loss of their baby by raising the topic with Leroy. She sees the community college as a place to get help.

Her mother is frightened by Norma Jean's growth and uses cruel comments about the baby's death to fight her. Mabel blames Norma Jean's change on the community college. "Her brain's all balled up over them books." All three characters use non-standard grammar and present-tense verbs when they speak, as uneducated people often do, implying they neither order the past nor plan for the future. When an energized Norma Jean tries to talk about her composition course, Leroy feels she is criticizing his English.

At first, Norma Jean encourages Leroy to join her in a fresh start at life, in the creation of a better marriage. He knows they must do this together if he is not to lose her, but he cannot stop resorting to his usual escape routes of smoking dope and avoiding all conflict. In an attempt to get Norma Jean "back in line," Mabel suggests a day-trip to the Civil War battlefield of Shiloh, where she spent her honeymoon thirty-five years ago. It does not help. By the end of Mason's short story, Norma Jean, although unclear about her motivation, announces she wants to leave Leroy.

"Shiloh" came at the beginning of the prolonged process I went through in conceptualizing this study. Seven years ago, I was discussing the story with one of my literature classes, maybe for the third or fourth time, when the thought passed through my mind that one character in it was at a community college. She is not taking college-credit courses, apparently, but at least she is enrolled at a two-year college. I did nothing with this thought except place it on a shelf somewhere in my head, even though I have taught at two-year colleges since the 1960s and attended a junior college during my own freshman year. Only later did it occur to me that after decades on a community college faculty, and even more decades of reading widely, Norma Jean Moffitt was the only fictional character I could remember, in any medium, who was associated with a two-year college.

I knew then that "Shiloh" was important in some way, and so I continued to include it on the literature course syllabus. Still later, maybe the next semester, I tried involving students in my discovery, thinking they would identify with Norma Jean. Instead, they distanced themselves as far from her as they could, especially those re-entry women that *I* saw as closest to her. I was surprised, and somewhat puzzled. What brought about our disagreement? Which of us was practicing denial? What did I think the students had in common with Norma Jean that they seemed to want to disavow? Was it because they feared their own growth and its impact on their lives, or was it because they were more perceptive than I was and felt that the author was looking down upon her characters?

More time passed, and I started to think about why the students did not want to identify with Norma Jean, and why, in some ways, they were correct not to. Finally, in the last phase of my extended and evolving learning process, I started on my present journey, the first step of which was to research American culture for more community college characters and to write articles about the fictional image of the two-year college in our society.

I emphasize this slow and hesitant dawning because, despite the fact that my own life experience should have persuaded me otherwise, my reluctance to see what was in front of me mirrors society's judgmental image of the two-year college and its millions of inhabitants. That is, we barely notice that the two-year college exists, and when it does surface, it is treated as "the polyester of higher education,"[2] slightly comical and meant for losers. A synthetic education, in other words, substituting for "real" college. And, like cheap and ordinary fabric, the two-year college phenomenon has never become a fashionable subject for writers or film-makers, even though over five million people each year choose to avail themselves of the two-year system. Poverty, racism, and many other low-status topics can be considered "trendy" from time to time, but never the community college.

Why did I not see earlier that two-year colleges were invisible in fiction, or, if noticed, usually maligned? I can hardly be surprised at society in general. I have long been a defender of the community college, justifying my job and my freshman year in the process. I have fairly good antennae for outrage. Was it the invisibility that threw me off? Was I accepting the power hierarchy and my place in it? Trying to be at least superior to my students?[3]

In a recent book on plate tectonics and continental drift, a geologist, trying to explain why the theory took so long to be accepted despite its proposal as early as the eighteenth century, quoted an old maxim: "The eye seldom sees what the mind does not anticipate."[4] The eye sees what it is trained to

---

[2] John Platt, unpublished letter to Nancy LaPaglia, February 1992.

[3] Herman Sinaiko, Committee on General Studies in the Humanities of the University of Chicago, in a discussion in August 1992, told me that this attitude, contempt for one's own students, is common today in universities and liberal arts colleges. To say, "The faculty is better [in quality] than the students," is considered a compliment to the college. Are two-year college faculties and staff simply aping their "betters?"

[4] John McPhee, "Annals of the Former World (Geology - Part II)," *The New Yorker*, 14 September 1992, 44.

see, in other words. Nature is not neat, but messy, and thus difficult to discern. Culture, one aspect of which I have tried to see and describe, is even messier.

Or perhaps I can give myself another excuse for not noticing earlier the invisibility and denigration of the two-year college. Stanley Crawford, a contemporary novelist and essayist, describes something he calls "philosophical gradualism," a slow accumulation of small changes arrived at "only by a long succession of small or even absentminded observations."[5] The observer fails to see the phenomenon for what it is, "so entangled is it in a habitual activity spread out over many years." I am that absentminded observer who took so long to see the contradiction between the "official" view and what I knew to be true from experience.

Whatever it was that kept me from seeing the contradiction for so long, it is time for me to examine it. Discovery is directed, and always has been directed, by what the culture thinks is important, says the narrator of *The Day the Universe Changed.*[6] Not many have thought the millions of people connected to two-year colleges significant enough to even notice, much less to value as important. Therefore, my purpose in this book is to address the discrepancy in the visibility and in the worth conferred upon the two-year college and its inhabitants by two kinds of storytellers. The storytellers I will examine are: (1) The writers of American fiction, including popular fiction and the mass media; and (2) thirty-seven students and faculty from community colleges who wrote about their experiences in journal format for my analysis.

---

[5] Stanley Crawford, *A Garlic Testament: Seasons on a Small New Mexico Farm* (New York: Harper Collins, 1992), 87.

[6] James Burke, "On the Origin of Species," *The Day the Universe Changed,* P.B.S., 1991, videocassette.

Over five million people this year alone, nearly half of all the undergraduates in the United States, are enrolled in junior or community colleges.[7] Almost one-half of all college faculty teach in two-year schools. Many of the students are closer to the margins of society than others attending college. Over sixty percent of all two-year college students are women, and these schools also enroll large percentages of minority, older, immigrant, poor, and other "non-traditional" students. (The non-traditional student has actually become the norm in many four-year colleges as well, but cultural mythology regarding higher education has not yet caught up with this development.)

If art is an accurate reflection of its time and place, then judging by American fiction, including the popular non-print media of television and movies, there should be very few people in two-year colleges. Those characters who occasionally appear in fiction are mediocre, probably losers, and usually unsympathetic. The prior research that I had done suggested that American fiction reflected the two-year college's lack of status in our cultural pattern, and not the actuality of its inhabitants. With rare exceptions, the students and faculty are not considered worth writing about, much less taking seriously. My own life experience as a teacher belies this judgement.

Therefore, I focused my investigation on the following groups of questions:

1. What is the image of the two-year college in American fiction? Why the scarcity of references to two-year college people, given the demographics of higher education in this

---

[7] All statistical information on two-year colleges and other educational institutions has been taken from *The Chronicle of Higher Education Abstracts*, August, 1991.

country? Why the usual belittling depiction when they do appear? Does this reflect society's message to the millions of community college inhabitants? Were there critical and historical junctures that shaped the fictional view of the two-year college?

2. Will the image presented by fiction's stock figure for the two-year college, a re-entry woman student, be different when she herself gets a chance to describe her own experience? Will the journal writers see themselves as losers or as winners, their colleges as delimiting or as enhancing? (As "Rinky-Dink College," as one writer put it, or as the way up?)[8]

3. What are the precise differences between the two views? Is the message that society itself sends, through its art forms and other means, an ironic contradiction? That is, does the message indicate that the "right thing to do" is to go to college and improve yourself, but the consequences are that you will be demeaned for doing it? Since the minority women who comprise a substantial percentage of the actual two-year college population are almost totally absent in fiction, will the image that they present in their journals differ from those of white women and/or from the fictional depiction?

4. What effect does the pejorative image have on two-year college inhabitants or on prospective students? Are two-year college students and faculty even *aware* of the popular negative conception? Does this phenomenon in itself discourage the very people who need the two-year colleges the most from entering the doors—those people on the margins of our society who can afford little else? Is the popular view an impediment to the success of those who do enter two-year colleges? Are these supposed "inferiors" influenced

---

[8] T. Glen Coughlin, *The Hero of New York* (New York: Norton, 1986).

by the view of others more highly placed in society and in our system of higher education?

5. If the fictional view of the two-year college discourages and demeans the very people who need the most help, is there any remedy for this situation? Even if fiction and the journals are looking at different people (a possible reason why they may differ so much), the ethical question remains: Why ignore or mock most two-year college inhabitants? Wouldn't society be better off if these people were not made to feel inferior? The idea underlying Plato's utopia in *The Republic*[9] is to treat everyone to make them better. Why would we want to live with people we have made worse?

Definitions

Storyteller: Anyone who tells a story. From the Latin for *history*.[10] A teller of happenings, whether true or fictitious. In the earliest meaning of the word, one who tells the true story. Later, a writer of fiction, as well. Now, possibly, a liar, or at least the implication that one is not telling the whole truth and nothing but. This study focuses on two kinds of storytellers: (1) the outsider, who is the professional fiction writer; and (2) the insider, who is the amateur autobiographer.

Image: From the Latin for *imitation*, a copy. Thus, I do not pretend to be studying "reality," but images held by various groups.

Insider: One who is within the limits of some organization, and thus in possession of special information. Possibly one who is "in on the secret." Thus, an "outsider" is one for

---

[9] Plato, *The Republic*, Book I (New York: Penguin Books, 1955).

[10] All general definitions of specific words are taken from *The Oxford English Dictionary* (Oxford: Oxford University Press, 1971).

whom an organization other than the two-year college constitutes the primary reference.

Fiction: Originally, that which is feigned, invented, or imagined. Now, it usually refers to a literary work. The dearth of fictional works that refer to two-year colleges, even by means of a single mention, is so profound that I am unable to afford the luxury of the narrowed definition that can be adopted by those who study the academic novel or other depictions of higher education. For example, some researchers of four-year college fiction treat only those works that are "set almost exclusively on a campus" or are "worthy of scholarly attention."[11] I cannot do this, nor is it my concern. In fact, popular fiction and passing references, especially in the mass media, may be the most influential in creating or reflecting images.

Returning women or re-entry women: Women students who did not go directly from a traditional-age high school graduation to college. These women were out of school at least four years and are at least twenty-two years of age. Although some of them may have come up through the G.E.D. or Adult Basic Education route at a two-year college, they have been in the college-credit system long enough to have passed English composition or its equivalent.

In most *fictional* representations, it is difficult or impossible to tell whether the creator or writer is referring to college credit courses or to some other two-year college function (e.g., remedial education). Therefore, I will count a fictional character as a two-year college student as long as the work refers to her or him as such.

---

[11] Barbara Vandermeer, "The Academic Novel as a Resource in the Study of Higher Education" (Ph.D. diss., University of Alabama, 1982), 164.

Women faculty: Women who teach full-time at a two-year college and have done so for at least four years.

Journal: A written record of one's own thoughts and experiences. It may be kept as a diary (a daily written record) or not. It is always autobiographical, although focused on a specific experience in this case, and it records personal observations.

Two-year college: A junior or community college. There are four categories of educational institutions in the United States that I *eliminated* in the search for two-year college characters in fiction:

1. The prep school junior college, e.g., Holden Caulfield's Pencey Prep College in *The Catcher in the Rye*, which has a photo of students playing polo on its brochure.[12]

2. Non-collegiate night school for adults, e.g., the Gentleman Caller's class in public speaking in *The Glass Menagerie*.[13]

3. Municipal Americanization classes, e.g., Hyman Kaplan's American Night Preparatory School for Adults, in *The Education of H*Y*M*A*N   K*A*P*L*A*N*.[14]

4. English as a Second Language classes or G.E.D. classes which may or may not be connected to a two-year college, e.g., the E.S.L. class in the film *El Norte*[15] or the G.E.D. class in one episode of the television series *Gimme a Break!*[16]

---

[12] J. D. Salinger, *The Catcher in the Rye* (New York: Little, Brown, 1945).

[13] Tennessee Williams, *The Glass Menagerie* (New York: New Directions, 1945).

[14] Leo Rosten, *The Education of H*Y*M*A*N   K*A*P*L*A*N* (New York: Harcourt Brace, 1937).

[15] *El Norte*, directed and produced by Gregory Nava and Anna Thomas, 1983, motion picture.

[16] "Gimme a Break!," 1991, television series.

Non-traditional student: In its broadest sense, anyone who doesn't fit the "traditional" pattern of being a full-time student, living on campus, and progressing straight through college without a break for family or career. The term is sometimes used to imply "multi-cultural" (that is, non-white, in today's euphemism) as well. At many American colleges and universities the percentage of "non-traditional" students is approaching half the total enrollment. In a community college, "non-traditional" students are usually in the majority. Enrollment trends suggest that the two-year colleges are simply ahead of "the fours."

Five Things I Am Not Trying to Do

1. I do not intend to argue the actual intellectual or other merits of two-year colleges versus other undergraduate schools. Two-year colleges are not elite, since in most cases they must admit those students who show up at their doors. This does not mean, however, that defining all their students as losers is an accurate reflection of our cultural pattern.

2. I do not intend to follow the relatively few academic researchers who have studied the two-year college, themselves almost all from universities. Their findings are not central to my concerns. I have read Brent and Karabel,[17] Clark,[18] Vaughan,[19] Jencks,[20] Orfield,[21] and others, and I do

---

[17]Stephen Brent and Jerome Karabel, *The Diverted Dream: Unfulfilled Promises of the Community College, 1904-85* (Oxford: Oxford University Press, 1989).

[18]Burton Clark, "The Cooling Out Function Revisited," in *Questioning the Community College Role. New Directions for Community Colleges*, no. 32. (San Francisco: Jossey-Bass, 1980), 15-31.

[19]George B. Vaughan, *The Community College in America* (Washington, DC: Community College Press, 1985).

not wish to do yet another investigation of the dismal failure of the two-year colleges and their inhabitants. I am not contradicting their work; I simply have another focus. According to Arthur Cohen, one of the less disparaging of the academics doing research on two-year colleges, there is very little educational criticism of the two-year college being done, especially from within the system.[22] I am a critic from within.

3. I will not discuss the actual function that a community college education fills in our society, although I agree with Orfield and others who have focused on the education of African-Americans. Those students who need the most help and are most likely to be unfamiliar with the ins and outs of higher education get the shortest end of every stick. The student journals support this view, as the African-American writers have the most serious complaints and are the least happy with the two-year college system.

4. Although the journals may contradict the pejorative image given in American fiction and by many academic writers, I am not trying to legitimize the ideological basis of our ruling class. The faculty members who wrote journals for me would be furious if I were to conclude this study as an apologist for the *status quo*, since they (and several of the students) are fighting just this hegemony at each of the five colleges in which they are located. (My own campus is a part of the City Colleges of Chicago, where the wealthy business-

---

[20] Christopher Jencks, *Inequality: A Reassessment of the Effect of Family and Schooling in America* (New York: Basic Books, 1972).

[21] Gary Orfield and others, *The Chicago Study of Access and Choice in Higher Education: A Report to the Illinois Senate Committee on Higher Education* (Chicago: University of Chicago Press, Committee on Public Policy Studies Research Project, 1984).

[22] Arthur Cohen, University of California at Los Angeles, in a conversation in Chicago, 2 May 1992.

man who heads the Board of Trustees has recently made the determination that our students are primarily deserving of factory training.)[23]

5. I am not entering the competition for who is the most victimized in our society. All victimization is unjust, the less profound as well as the most damaging. This study is not an exercise in provoking pity. I am not presenting two-year college inhabitants as the wretched of the earth, but as people who are considered worth less than others in society's common view. Their stories have not been heard, and I intend to listen to them.

Therefore, what I *will* be doing is looking at two sources that are not usually considered in research concerning the two-year college, even though one of my sources, fiction, is powerfully effective in creating images. How well do these sources reflect the complexity of reality? As Annie Dillard writes in *Living by Fiction*, "Our knowledge is contextual and only contextual."[24] I am trying to describe a phenomenon, the image of the two-year college, within the context I know best.

After this book was completed, I read what I could have used as an academic model for my methodology. A new book, *Slim's Table: Race, Respectability, and Masculinity*, is a sociological study of about thirty working-class African-American men who eat at a cafeteria in my own neighborhood on the South Side.[25] It was originally a Ph.D. dissertation at the University of Chicago. The author's findings contradict the

---

[23]Nancy Millman, "Crash Course," *Chicago* (September 1992), 110-13, 132-34. Mr. Gidwitz's attitude can be seen perhaps more clearly in various interviews he has given to Chicago newspapers and in directives and letters he has sent to the faculty of the City Colleges of Chicago.

[24]Annie Dillard, *Living by Fiction* (New York: Harper & Row, 1982), 149.

[25]Mitchell Duneier, *Slim's Table: Race, Respectability, and Masculinity* (Chicago: University of Chicago Press, 1992).

social stereotypes usually applied to non-middle class African-American men by respected social scientists of all races, as well as by the media and by society in general. The author based his conclusions on an analysis of the men's conversations with him and on his own observations over a period of several years.

Among many laudatory reviews the book has received, one from a Berkeley academic says, "It shakes up the distorted media and social science images of black men and black class structure: Duneier restores visibility to these solid working class men."[26] The men themselves, his subjects, are sensitive about the pejorative images they see in popular fiction, "because they know that the society they live in, from its best sociologists to its funniest comedians, associates them with similar stereotypes." I see many parallels to my own study in this work, and perhaps I can accomplish even a small "shake-up" for another group of Americans and for their milieu, the two-year college.

The Design of the Study

In a one-sentence synopsis: I investigated a stereotype, and then found actual people who were living in the stereotype's situation in order to see what they had to say about the experience. That is, I examined the stories of two kinds of storytellers: The writers of American fiction, including popular fiction and the mass media; and thirty-seven students and faculty who wrote about their experiences in journal format specifically for my study.

---

[26]Bob Blauner, University of California at Berkeley, quoted on the jacket of *Slim's Table*.

A thematic analysis of both kinds of literature uncovered "different maps of the same geography,"[27] maps perhaps so incongruous that my analysis may be a way to "critique the media by which we in the U.S. are taught." Or, to use another metaphor, if all that a future historian (or sociologist or Martian) understood about the two-year college system came from the data I collected, what would she know? When these data are approached without an established theoretical framework in mind, what common themes emerge?

For the location of the fictional references, I began an extensive search six years ago, which was much increased in intensity in the past two years. In addition to library research, this inquiry involved hundreds of questionnaires and notices in publications such as *The Chronicle of Higher Education* and elsewhere. I wrote to all of the writers I found who ever used a reference to a two-year college, asking them for additional leads in their own work or that of others.

For the autobiographical material, thirty-seven open-ended journals were written at my request by twenty-three re-entry women students and fourteen women faculty from five community colleges in Illinois, Oregon, and New York. There were follow-up interviews of two students and one faculty member from Illinois, in order to question them specifically about a theme that occurred in every other journal but theirs.

I will take up the interesting question of what I did *not* find in American fiction in the concluding chapter—that is, the phenomenon of near invisibility of the two-year college

---

[27]Rhonda Robinson, "How Can You 'Know' if You Can't Control? New Research Issues in Instructional Technology," a paper presented at the fifth annual LEPS Department awards convocation, Northern Illinois University, October 1991.

and its inhabitants. The question of invisibility is related, of course, to the negative nature of the image when it surfaces. What is considered to be not worth noticing is not going to be praised when it makes an occasional appearance.

Using a similar process in *Revolution from Within*, Gloria Steinem combined her research on self-esteem with women's personal stories, which are, she says, "like all accounts of any group that has been marginalized, our best textbooks: the only way to make our experience central."[28] Or, as Phyllis Cunningham writes, "I think ordinary people can define their own problems," instead of depending on problem definition done by elites from the university and elsewhere.[29] This is why I needed another view, that of the usually unheard people who live the experience that fiction and academia malign.

Literature as Data

Fiction is my friend. It has been my friend since childhood, and it bothers me to argue with it. I can contradict scholars and experts without much trouble, but I am of the opinion common to many in the humanities that fiction is a repository of truth. However, in this book, I take the view that fiction, if not actually dead wrong, ignores large areas that are central to the experience it purports to depict.

Using literature as data is not uncommon. Sharan Merriam,[30] Alan Quigley,[31] Donald Polkinghorne,[32] and others in

---

[28]Gloria Steinem, *Revolution from Within: A Book of Self-Esteem* (Boston: Little, Brown, 1992), 4.

[29]Phyllis Cunningham, "Own Your Advocacy," *Adult Learning Magazine*, November 1990, 19.

[30]Sharan Merriam, *Themes of Adulthood Through Literature* (New York: Teachers College Press, Columbia University, 1983).

education and related fields have done so with interesting results. Elizabeth Hill, whose work at the University of Iowa was so helpful to me, investigated fiction about re-entry women in higher education.[33] "In many ways," she says, "reading about an event can be similar to actually experiencing it."[34]

Other writers warn of the dangers of looking to literature for truth. Annie Dillard, in *Living by Fiction*, says that "Fiction is fabrication . . . an ordering or rearrangement of selected materials from the actual world. Art prizes originality more than fidelity. It is a terrible interpreter."[35] A much earlier humanist, Plato, crowned the writers in his utopia with laurel wreaths to honor them and then escorted them to the gates of the city. Their beautiful lies were too convincing.[36]

I believe that all art is a reflection of the *ideas* of its time and place, if not the reality, or at least of the ideas of those who pay for art's production. The greater the writer (or visual artist or composer), the more likely that the specific circumstances and values of a culture or patron might be transcended. For example, Tolstoi said some things about dying in *The Death of Ivan Ilych* that, if not universal, apply more widely than only to nineteenth-century Russians or to upper-

---

[31] Alan Quigley, "The Resisters: An Analysis of Non-Participation in Adult Basic Education" (Ed.D. diss., Northern Illinois University, 1987).

[32] Donald Polkinghorne, *Narrative Knowing and the Human Sciences* (Albany, NY: State University of New York Press, 1988).

[33] Elizabeth Hill, "A Study of Re-entry Women in Fiction and Research: A Comparative Analysis" (Ph.D. diss., University of Iowa, 1990).

[34] Elizabeth Hill, "Literary Research and the Study of Re-Entry Women," *Continuing Higher Education* 37, no. 2 (Spring 1989): 9.

[35] Dillard, *Living by Fiction*, 178.

[36] Plato, *The Republic*, Book X, trans. Desmond Lee (New York: Penguin Books, 1955).

class men.[37] In the same work, he reflects a view of marriage, or of marriageable women, that seems closely allied to the prevailing belief system of the powerful in his time.

Which is true of the writers who depict the two-year college—transcendence or duplication? I am assuming that some of each occurs, but my focus here, once again, is on image, and not on reality. I may not have found the Tolstoi of the two-year college, but I took what I could find, and I believe that it reflects commonly held views. In any case, in my search of the academic literature I could not find another analysis of the two-year college in fiction, although there are many such works on four-year colleges and universities.[38] It is time that someone started the investigation.

Open-Ended Journals as Data

A search of the academic literature did not turn up the use of journals written specifically as data for a study, although in some ways the format is similar to open-ended interviews, which are commonly used. What I wanted to do was create another body of literature, one that could be contrasted with the fiction. Autobiographies can be consid-

---

[37]Leo Tolstoi, "The Death of Ivan Ilych," in *The Short Novels of Tolstoi* (New York: Dial Press, 1946), 409-70.

[38]A few examples follow: John E. Kramer, Jr., *The American College Novel* (New York: Garland, 1981); John O. Lyons, *The College Novel in America* (Carbondale, IL: Southern Illinois University Press, 1962); Von Pittman and John Theilmann, "The Administrator in Fiction: Portrayals of Higher Education," *Educational Forum*, 50, no. 4 (Summer 1986): 405-18; John Thelin and Barbara Townsend, "Fiction to Fact: College Novels and the Study of Higher Education," in *Higher Education: Handbook of Theory and Research*, 4 (New York: Agathon Press, 1988).

ered as literature, even when brief and narrowly focused. Therefore, open-ended journals served my purpose.

Why were the journals totally open-ended, both in format and in content? I backed into the method by chance and by good fortune, while trying to correlate the journals with the fiction. I could not tell Joyce Carol Oates or Saul Bellow what to write about or how to write, so why tell the journal writers? I would take what I found, in the journals as in the fiction, and see what came up.

I believe that this method produced results that can be taken seriously, even though I cannot generalize from them. "In an unstructured interview, ideas get out on the subject's terms."[39] The same is true of an unstructured journal. It is one thing to ask, with subtlety or otherwise, "In what way are you aware of your marginality, and what if anything have you done about it?" or "Do you ever feel the joy of learning?" It is altogether another thing to have thirty-six out of thirty-seven writers bring up the topic of marginality or the joy of learning without prompting. I discovered this phenomenon when I analyzed the journals, and thus it was more credible to consider the themes I found as indicative of the actual images held by the people who wrote for me. In addition, the open-ended format made it more possible to approach the data with few preconceived themes or theories, since I did not have to decide what I was looking for before reading the data.

---

[39] Jim Thomas, Sociology Department, Northern Illinois University, during a classroom lecture, July, 1991.

Method of Analysis

I did a content analysis of both sets of "documents," grouping and comparing emergent themes, in order to arrive at a description of the two-year college from two differing perspectives. I spoke with each of the journal writers, sometimes briefly, before they wrote, and kept notes on those meetings. Three of the thirty-seven writers were interviewed at length several months after they wrote, and those interviews were included in the analysis.

In the chapters that follow, I offer a kind of narrative collage taken from a compilation of the data. For example, a picture of the two-year college is presented as one might see it in American fiction that depicts community college students. Still another picture is given of the two-year college, one that comes out of fourteen autobiographies written by women faculty.

"All qualitative research is textual analysis."[40] I looked for conflicts of meaning within each "document," and between groups of documents. I used several points of view in my data base: fiction writers, community college students, community college faculty, academic researchers, and my own life experience. Point of view colors everything we do. I did not assume any kind of neutrality on the part of any one point of view. The world of the two-year college, like the rest of the world in which it exists, has been socially constructed.[41]

---

[40]Paul Ilsley, LEPS Department, Northern Illinois University, during a classroom lecture, July, 1992.

[41]Peter L. Berger and Thomas Luckmann, *The Social Construction of Reality: A Treatise in the Sociology of Knowledge* (New York: Doubleday, 1967). For a more recent treatment of the same idea, see Toni Morrison, ed., *Race-ing Justice, En-gendering Power: Essays on Anita Hill, Clarence Thomas, and the Construction of Social Reality* (New York: Pantheon, 1992).

Any particular image of it held by a group of people or by an individual comes out of that construct.

Significance to the Field of Adult Education

The contradiction between insider and outsider images of the two-year college is not a topic that should remain invisible, since it involves a disturbing disregard for the fastest-growing segment of higher education in the United States today. Society's negative definition of the millions of two-year college students and faculty does them unwarranted violence. Thus, it is imperative to write about the phenomenon and to make some portions of the "map" more visible. Only some values have been reflected; only some stories have been heard. Ways must be developed for the many neglected stories to be addressed by adult educators and others.

My intended audience includes at least three groups:

1. All two-year college inhabitants, including former and *future* two-year college students, and perhaps particularly all those who work at two-year colleges and take pride in what they do

2. Writers of fiction, especially those who work in popular culture and mass media, and, even more especially, those who have not actually experienced the two-year college from the inside

3. A general thoughtful public, and particularly for feminists, in some ways that are very important to me personally.

The white working-class woman, the stereotype two-year college student in fiction, may be the last woman on earth who can be "correctly" treated without dignity by feminists and others who are customarily very careful about their political language. I have encountered this form of snobbery often in the past. "She's overweight, she wears polyester pant

suits, she's a racist." This stereotyping and the two-year
college are closely linked in the imagery of some outsiders,
and both the women and the colleges suffer from each other's
low status. The low esteem in which they are held makes it
difficult to convince many academics, including feminists, to
take them seriously or sympathetically, or even to consider
them as objects of study.

Since I regard myself a member, at least a fringe member,
of both sides—feminists and researchers on the one hand, and
two-year college and working-class people on the other—I
would like to gather them into one circle. They could see how
much they have in common and how similar their stories are,
similar at least in their capacity to move their readers and
illuminate experience.

Early versions of two of the chapters that follow produced the reactions that I think I was looking for. I will report
two separate responses. In the first, a prominent feminist
leader in Illinois read the chapter on the usual demeaning view
of the two-year college student that is found in fiction. This
reader said it was "like getting hit up-side the head," when
she realized that she herself had previously dismissed these
people, the very women to whose improved circumstances
she is devoting her life. What an exceptionally honest person
she is to admit this out loud! In the other example, a two-year
college faculty member read the chapter analyzing the faculty
journals. When she finished, she had tears in her eyes because
someone had finally validated what she had spent her life
doing, receiving little recognition for it other than that of some
grateful students.

This is what I wish to do in this book: hit some people
"up-side the head" and recognize the worth of those who have
been unacknowledged.

Chapter 2

The Single-Mention List[1]

In some parts of South America, armadillos grow to almost
five feet in length and are allowed to teach at the
junior-college level.

Donald Barthelme, "Lightning"[2]

During my search for references to two-year colleges in
American fiction, I developed what I call a *single
mention* list. That is, I compiled an inventory of short stories,
novels, films or fictional television programs that refer to a
community or junior college just once. I began to notice that
when this occurs, there is a specific usage in mind. "Community college" and "junior college" have become shorthand for
a long inventory of pejorative, demeaning adjectives.

In much the same way, the mention of certain cities or
towns used to be a shorthand way for comedians of indicating

---

[1] This chapter reprinted with permission by the Community College
Humanities Association. Nancy LaPaglia, "The Single Mention List," *Community
College Humanities Review,* 13 (December 1992): 61-66.

[2] Donald Barthelme, "Lightning," in *Forty Stories* (New York: Penguin
Books, 1987), 177.

people who were hicks, backwater, even dim-witted. A two-year college character in fiction has become a synonym for a loser, a clown, someone who is not to be taken seriously. This fictional character is more likely to be a student, rather than a member of the faculty or staff, and she is usually a working-class white woman and a re-entry student, a woman older than the "traditional" age. She is rarely a *minority* working-class woman, even though many attend two-year schools.

I'll begin with single-mentions in novels. In Jill Eisenstadt's *From Rockaway*, a group of bored young lifeguards try to break away from the banality of "Rotaway," New York.[3] One female failure winds up at the local community college. In Gloria Naylor's *The Women of Brewster Place*, a middle-class young African-American who sees herself as a revolutionary enrolls part-time in a community college, precisely because such a school has no status, and thus she need not apologize for being upwardly mobile.[4] In another Barthelme work, *Paradise*, three direction-less beauties survey their chances for a better life.[5] One has one and a half "ragged years" at a community college; they all realize this does not improve her odds in the least. In Walter Walker's *The Immediate Prospect of Being Hanged*, the central character enrolls at Walmouth Junior College, located in an eastern state, instead of going to Vietnam.[6] His father wanted him to go to a "good" college like Yale, and when the student receives *B* grades the first semester without going to class, the father gets

---

[3] Jill Eisenstadt, *From Rockaway* (New York: Alfred Knopf, 1987).

[4] Gloria Naylor, *The Women of Brewster Place* (New York: Penguin Books, 1982).

[5] Donald Barthelme, *Paradise* (New York: Putnam, 1986).

[6] Walter Walker, *The Immediate Prospect of Being Hanged* (New York: Viking, 1989).

him a job as an insurance adjuster. In the opinion of the novel's narrator, the junior college was a school for draft-dodgers, re-entry women and the very dumb.

Short stories provide similar material. In Ella Leffland's "Last Courtesies," a gum-snapping, stereo-blasting young hooker is "taking macrame and World Lit. at the jay cee."[7] Her boyfriend, a serial murderer known as the Rain Man, tells us this. In Lee Smith's "Bob, A Dog," a beautician's husband teaches at the community college "instead of having a real job."[8] She herself is a loser; when he wishes to become more trendy, he leaves her for a frizzy-haired math teacher who jogs.

The New Yorker printed Alan Sternberg's "Moose."[9] Moose works at the dump. His dream is to move up to a large landfill machine. He takes introductory chemistry at Middle-sex Community College. He will fail, in the course and in life. In "The Deer Leg Chronicle" by R. D. Jones, a crazed young man is terrorizing a North Carolina town by breaking things with a deer leg.[10] (He had started out with a rabbit's foot at age five, and worked his way up.) Eventually, he mends his ways and gets a job in a shoe store, but not before trying to break the storm door of Marsha, a student he met in a chemistry class he was taking at Surry Community College.

I found single mentions in one play and one poem. In Lynn Siefert's *Little Egypt*, a nerdy daughter in a battling

---

[7] Ella Leffland, "Last Courtesies," in *Last Courtesies and Other Stories* (New York: Harper & Row, 1980), 141.

[8] Lee Smith, "Bob, A Dog," in *Me and My Baby View the Universe* (New York: Ballantine, 1990), 21.

[9] Alan Sternberg, "Moose," *The New Yorker*, 12 September 1988.

[10] R. D. Jones, "The Deer Leg Chronicle," *Southern Magazine*, February 1989, 46, 56-57.

family is called "Egghead" because of her year at a local junior college.[11] Unlike her sexy sister, she loves to read. *The History of Penicillin* is a favorite. She finds happiness with a local goof. Donald Hall's *Six Poets in Search of a Lawyer* describes a junior college teacher named Dullard who is overpraised as a new Homer in his ignorant milieu.[12]

Murder mysteries currently are excellent sources. In Valerie Miner's *Murder in the English Department*, a non-tenured woman on the Berkeley English faculty imagines in her worst nightmare that she is exiled to Natchez Junior College.[13] Her non-academic clod of a brother-in-law thinks the local community college is good enough for his bright daughter, as it was for his empty-headed daughters-in-law. Ms. Berkeley will rescue the daughter, for a happy ending.

Carolyn Hart's *A Little Class on Murder* is an interesting single mention, because the mention appears only on the *cover* of the paperback.[14] Because the class in question has some older women students and the subject matter of the course is popular culture, the cover refers to Chastain Community College, even though the college has an M.A. program, students who get Fulbrights, publish-or-perish faculty, and other accoutrements not usually found in two-year schools. And it is never once called a community college in the book.

---

[11] Lynn Siefert, *Little Egypt*, play performed at Steppenwolf Theatre, Chicago, December 1987.

[12] Donald Hall, "Six Poets in Search of a Lawyer," in *Exiles and Marriages* (New York: Viking, 1955), 61.

[13] Valerie Miner, *Murder in the English Department* (New York: St. Martin's Press, 1982).

[14] Carolyn Hart, *A Little Class on Murder* (New York: Bantam, 1989).

Charles Willeford, in *Miami Blues* and other hard-boiled mysteries, uses two-year college references more than once.[15] In *The Burnt Orange Heresy*, two young women, students at Palm Beach Junior College, take notes at an art gallery opening.[16] The mention seems unusually neutral, and the two play no other part in the story. In Joan Hess's *Strangled Prose*, a faculty member at a small liberal arts college who is a militant feminist and a suspected lesbian is asked to leave.[17] "At this point I'm praying for a backwater junior college to at least read my résumé," she says. She compares the two-year college to Greenland, "a swan dive into academic obscurity."

Fiction that occurs in non-print media offers more illustrations. In the movie *Maid to Order*, a spoiled young woman, formerly wealthy but now poor, argues that she did not spend six years at a junior college in order to become a maid[18] In *Sibling Rivalry*, a woman who is married to a rich surgeon advises the flaky and poorer sister she considers hopeless, that she could go to a community college.[19] In the film *The Bonfire of the Vanities*,[20] as well as in Tom Wolfe's novel,[21] an African-American young man has been run over. His high school English teacher sets an interviewer straight about what it means to be an honors student and go on to college in the

---

[15] Charles Willeford, *Miami Blues* (New York: Ballantine, 1984).

[16] Charles Willeford, *The Burnt Orange Heresy* (New York: Crown Publications, 1971).

[17] Joan Hess, *Strangled Prose* (New York: Ballantine, 1986), 108.

[18] *Maid to Order*, directed and produced by Amy Jones and Herb Jaffe, 1987, motion picture.

[19] *Sibling Rivalry*, directed and produced by Carl Reiner and Liz Glotzer, 1990, motion picture.

[20] *The Bonfire of the Vanities*, directed and produced by Brian DePalma, 1990, motion picture.

[21] Tom Wolfe, *The Bonfire of the Vanities* (New York: Farrar, Straus, 1987).

victim's milieu. "Honors" means you caused no trouble, and a community college is not a "real" college.

Now that attending a two-year college has been a mass cultural pattern for over a quarter of a century, some fictional examples can be found on television. Most of them are not single mentions, since an entire skit or episode may revolve around a community college situation. Some of the mentions are actually positive in nature. There is, however, psychologist Dr. Crane on *Cheers*, who reacts in horror at the suggestion he may wind up teaching at a two-year school.[22] At a later point, he indicates he would rather be damned than teach at a community college. And when television programs mention that a minor character attends, or plans to attend, a two-year school, that character is not usually a mental heavyweight.

To mention a two-year college connection imposes a negative filter on the person or event being described, and so it may be deleted out of "kindness." Gloria Steinem, in her recent book on self-esteem, *Revolution from Within*, discusses the made-for-TV movie *Nobody's Child* at length, without ever mentioning that the central character, her rescuers, and her academic mentors are all either students or faculty at a community college.[23] In this case, I am assuming that Steinem did not wish to inflict the negative filter on these admirable characters, since their story is meant to be inspirational.

Are there positive examples to counter the trend? Of course. But not many of them. The entire list of fictional works that refer to two-year colleges is short, especially when compared to the thousands of examples mentioning four-year

---

[22]"Cheers," 1991, television series.

[23]Gloria Steinem, *Revolution from Within: A Book of Self-Esteem* (Boston: Little Brown, 1992); *Nobody's Child*, directed by Lee Grant, 1986, made-for-TV motion picture.

colleges and universities. No researcher need bother with a single mention list there. Hundreds of novels, for example, are actually *set* in a four-year school; I have found only one novel set in a two-year school, Dorothy Bryant's *Ella Price's Journal*.[24] Perhaps the last section of Nancy Pelletier's *The Rearrangement* qualifies as a second example,[25] and the murder mystery *The Nominative Case* as a third.[26] Luckily, I was able to locate about three dozen other works of fiction that treat the two-year college in some way, even though it is not used as the major setting.

Why is "community college" shorthand for less than mediocre? I suspect for the same reasons that two-year colleges are deemed hardly worth writing about in the first place. They are full of "non-traditional," low-status people. These are people closer to the margins: working-class, women, minority groups, older, recent immigrants, or the urban poor (or the rural poor, for that matter). They have little appeal to writers, unless they are shooting each other or dealing dope or saving the farm. The millions of middle-class whites who are also attending two-year colleges, quietly trying to improve their lives, are equally ignored or mocked.

Why is it still acceptable, or even fashionable, to belittle community college people, especially if they are white, working-class women? It is curious that these women are demeaned for trying to do something that might easily be viewed positively. Are writers maintaining their own elite status at the two-year college's expense, or reflecting a culture that wishes to do this? Does a post-modern stance see com-

---

[24]Dorothy Bryant, *Ella Price's Journal* (Berkeley, CA: ATA Books, 1972).

[25]Nancy Pelletier, *The Rearrangement* (New York: Macmillan, 1985).

[26]Edward Mackin, *The Nominative Case* (New York: Walker & Company, 1991).

munity college people as hopelessly naive, trying to preserve optimistic traditional values? Or is it simply easier to use trite metaphors?

More to the point, for me, can this narrow view of the community college be made fuller, and thus a closer reflection of the actual people involved? Those who write could provide me with a *second* single mention list, one that is more positive. I will end this discussion of single-mentions with two examples from popular culture—murder mysteries—that could begin that second list. Texas author Bill Crider, in *Shotgun Saturday Night*, mentions once that the new woman deputy, who will soon prove herself to be competent and effective, got her A.A. in law enforcement from a community college near Houston.[27] And in Chicago, Mike Raleigh, in *Death in Uptown*, mentions Truman College only in passing. We never meet a character connected to it, but the school stands as a helpful presence in a neighborhood that needs a lot of assistance.[28] Both writers are in community college English departments, and they are familiar with the more positive aspects of re-entry white women and other two-year college inhabitants.

Can this narrow view of the two-year college be broadened, enriched to become a fuller reflection of the actual people involved? With over five million students now enrolled, and staffed by close to one half of all college teachers, surely two-year schools can provide other writers with some entries for Single Mention List #2: Community Colleges are for Winners.

---

[27] Bill Crider, *Shotgun Saturday Night* (New York: Walker & Company, 1987).

[28] Michael Raleigh, *Death in Uptown* (New York: St. Martin's Press, 1991).

Chapter 3

Two-Year College Students in Fiction

Norma Jean used to say, "If I lose ten minutes' sleep, I just
drag all day." Now she stays up late, writing compositions.
She got a B on her first paper—a how-to theme on
soup-based casseroles.

Bobbie Ann Mason, "Shiloh"[1]

Two-year college inhabitants rarely appear in fiction,
not even in the mass culture media of television and
movies. In the works where they do surface, the depiction is
likely to be demeaning and belittling. At this point, I would
like to discuss the fictional portrayals I located during my
search of several years, beginning with characters who are
two-year college students.

---

[1] Mason, "Shiloh," 11.

Not including twenty-five single mentions (and twenty-two leads to television programs I have not actually seen myself), I have found thirty-eight fictional works that include two-year college characters. Ten of them have faculty characters only, so that this discussion will concern the remaining twenty-eight, those which include students. I will discuss the faculty characters in Chapter 5.

The works about students include ten novels, six television programs, four murder mysteries, three movies, two short stories, two plays, and a semi-autobiography. Their publication or presentation dates range from 1945 to 1992, and the fictional time portrayed ranges from the 1930s to the present.

The archetypical character, the stock figure, in these works is a white, working class, woman of "non-traditional" college age, who attends college part-time. (We will see in Chapter 5 that her archetypical teacher is a white male in the English Department, although I did not know this when I began this study.) Three-fourths of the students are female, over 80 percent are white, and over 70 percent can be described as working class. Only five of the twenty-eight went to college directly from high school, so that fiction about community college students offers a way to write about "older" people in higher education. (I say "older," because a number of these re-entry students are in their mid- to-late twenties.)

Over 60 percent attend college part time. Their field of study varies greatly, but is most often unknown. The largest number (ten) are studying English, but this is probably a result of the other stock character in these stories—the male English teacher. Geographically, they are scattered throughout the United States in fourteen different states, in colleges located in both rural and in urban areas. Only seven of the twenty-eight authors of this fiction are white women themselves, so the stereotype is not simply a reflection of the writer's own situation.

Before the 1970s

Fictional references earlier than the 1970s are extremely rare. I have located a book from 1945,[2] one from 1953,[3] and one published in 1969.[4] The central characters in both of the earlier works are children of poor immigrants, unable to afford anything but their local junior college. Both live in major cities that have several four-year colleges they cannot afford to attend. Augie March's relatives are Eastern European Jews; Jade Snow Wong's are Cantonese. Both students can transfer, well prepared, to a major university after graduation from the junior college; their two-year school is the "People's College" in the traditional American myth of access to higher education. Both were students in the 1930s, he at Crane Junior College (the first of the City Colleges of Chicago), she at the just-opened San Francisco Junior College.

College experience is a relatively minor part of Saul Bellow's *The Adventures of Augie March*, but episodes involving what the author calls "the municipal college" weave in and out of the novel six or seven times. Augie's brother Simon first enters in order to prepare for a Civil Service test. Both brothers would have gone to work full time instead of attending any school, but the Depression eliminated that option. Bellow praises the college in one lengthy passage as

---

[2] Jade Snow Wong, *Fifth Chinese Daughter* (New York: Harper & Row, 1945).

[3] Saul Bellow, *The Adventures of Augie March* (New York: Viking, 1953).

[4] Joyce Carol Oates, *Them* (New York: Ballantine, 1969).

a "city-sponsored introduction to higher notions, Shakespeare and enough math to take the Civil Service exam." Multi-cultural, its student body includes African-Americans, Mexican-Americans, and others from across the city. The idea of going there is to become Americanized and educated; it is where "poor boys starve for eight years in order to become professionals." There are women students as well, but Bellow, as usual when he writes about women, is disparaging. He says that they, seemingly more middle class than the male students, are only there to look for husbands.

Other than the March brothers, we meet only one two-year college student as an individual. He is Manuel Padilla, an impoverished Mexican math genius, who transfers to the University of Chicago on a scholarship from the physics department, after obtaining his A.A. He and Augie steal textbooks "ordered" from them by faculty and graduate students at the local universities, but by the end of the novel they are no longer thieves. Manny is working in the bio-physics lab, and Augie, who will begin the University of Chicago in the spring, works in his brother's coal yard. Bellow makes it clear that Crane Junior College was a "real" college, successfully giving its students an education *and* upward mobility.

Fifth Chinese Daughter, by Jade Snow Wong, is catalogued in most libraries and bookstores under "juvenile fiction." It is actually an autobiography, written in the third-person singular style traditional in Chinese literature, and with most of the actual names changed. Its approach is straightforward and direct; its subject is Jade Snow Wong's life from early childhood to not long after college graduation. Now that multi-cultural education and ethnic writers have become popular, the book is undergoing a revival. It was re-printed in 1989 by the University of Washington Press.

The jacket of the original edition offers a good example of the invisibility of the two-year college. The blurb contains a synopsis of the central character's life, but it eliminates her junior college years between high school and Mills College and gives Mills credit for what actually happened at San Francisco Junior College—the excitement of "first feeling her way toward personal identity in the face of parental indifference and outright opposition." The publisher may have thought that a junior college background would not attract buyers or readers, and so misrepresented the actual story.

Jade Snow, a superior student, wanted to attend the University of California at Berkeley, but Chinese daughters were not sent to college, especially fifth daughters in a still-growing family. She was reluctant to attend a junior college when a friend recommended it, but went anyway in order to save her dream of Berkeley. She did very well and could have transferred to the university, but chose Mills College instead because of the full scholarship they offered her.

She is a science student at the junior college at first, until a sociology teacher astounds her with ideas about the different mores and standards that exist in the world. She sees for the first time that she can become an individual, a scholar, even a writer. Also, she becomes more American without dropping her Chinese culture and values. As the commencement speaker at her graduation, she credits the junior college for opening up her life in positive ways. Her parents, who do not speak any English, recognize her accomplishments for the first time and surprise and please her by taking her English teacher to a Chinese restaurant in celebration.

In the 1950s, the State Department had this book translated and widely distributed in seven Asian countries, hoping to show that the U.S. was so free and open a society that "even

a female born to poor Chinese immigrants could gain a
toehold."[5] There were editions published in Germany and
England as well. How ironic that one result of Wong's writing
was that the two-year college system, which generally gets
ignored or receives low marks in its own culture, reached
many readers beyond the United States and helped them gain
insight into the "People's College" system.

Both Bellow and Wong portray the original "dream" that
many academic studies, including Brent and Karabel's *The
Diverted Dream*, argue was sidetracked, if not destroyed, by
later developments in the two-year college system.[6] In reality,
the Augie Marches and the Jade Snow Wongs are still suc-
ceeding in two-year schools; those of us who teach in community colleges see them every semester. The "diversion"
that has been occurring since the early 1960s added millions
of people and dollars to other purposes and programs, with
an inevitable dilution of focus and success rate. In addition,
the two-year college system grew with extraordinary speed,
and thus became much more visible and perhaps also more
threatening to the traditional areas of higher education. I
believe that the fiction I found reflects this historic change.

The View From the 1970s

I did not locate a single portrayal of the two-year college
that appeared during the next sixteen years, the years that
include the watershed transition period between "junior" and
"community" colleges. The name change that most two-year
colleges went through was indicative of a change in function,

---

[5] From the introduction by the author to the re-issue of Jade Snow Wong, *Fifth
Chinese Daughter* (Seattle, WA: University of Washington Press, 1989), viii.

[6] Brent and Karabel, *The Diverted Dream.*

a shift from a clear focus on providing the first two years of a baccalaureate degree, to the creation of large multi-purpose community-centered institutions that included non-college level tasks like teaching adult literacy and providing short-term occupational courses for the general population. Those tasks were performed in our society earlier, of course, but generally not by two-year colleges.

One of the effects of the shift was to create some confusion in the public mind, if not in the minds of the two-year colleges as well. At the beginning of this chapter, when various demographic characteristics of the fictional students were listed, I did not include the percentage of those who were taking college-credit courses and those who were not, because it is often impossible to tell which category the author meant, or whether the author even makes any distinction between categories of courses in a two-year college.

Sixteen years after the publication of *The Adventures of Augie March*, the next work that appeared was Joyce Carol Oates's *Them*. It has a central character who fits every aspect of the stereotype. Maureen is a white, working-class, re-entry woman attending a two-year college part time. At twenty-six, she attempts some control of her future by enrolling in a night class at Highland Park Junior College. She has heard that the school is easier than the University of Detroit, where she flunked out some years earlier. Her life up to now has been saturated with unrelieved grimness and violence, and her neighborhood is filled with tired and helpless people. She is an indifferent student. She decides to marry her English instructor as part of a self-improvement plan, although he is already married and has three children. They marry. His life changes little, outside of feeling more guilt, but her rise in status enables her to turn her back on her terrible past and her dismal family. The entire situation is depressing and bleak.

In the early 1970s, late in his career, William Inge, the successful playwright of *Picnic* and other dramas, wrote two unsuccessful novels. One of them, *Good Luck, Miss Wyckoff*, concerns a sensitive but frustrated high school Latin teacher of thirty-seven who has a destructive affair with an African-American junior college jock.[7] He is one of the very rare minority students I found, and the novel has the only treatment I located of the routine practice of importing urban gladiators for sports teams, a custom especially common in Kansas and other Midwestern "jucos." These young men are usually African-American and are unable to qualify academically at four-year schools. They are paid to play, and they hope to bring up their grades in order to transfer to a four-year college. Their dream is to play on a professional team.

In this novel, the student is lonely, angry, aggressive, and controlling. Miss Wyckoff is obsessed by him, although he humiliates her repeatedly. They are caught one afternoon during a sexual torture episode in her high-school classroom. She is fired in disgrace and must leave town; thus the origin of the title, a good luck farewell from her colleagues, who wish her well. She asks that her former lover be allowed to continue in college, but she needn't have worried. No punishment will come to him; the coach tells her he'll be OK after the first touchdown.

The work that was most often cited by my correspondents as the place to look for two-year college characters is Dorothy Bryant's *Ella Price's Journal*.[8] Written entirely in the form of a journal assignment for a Bay City Junior College English class, its central character fits the stereotypical pattern in almost every respect. In addition, a new pattern emerges in

---

[7] William Inge, *Good Luck, Miss Wyckoff* (Boston: Little, Brown, 1970).

[8] Bryant, *Ella Price's Journal*.

the works that concern re-entry women students. The 1970s women are "punished" in some way for daring to break traditional patterns by returning to school, usually by the loss of their husbands and the alienation of their families. In Ella Price's case, both "punishments" occur, as well as the loss of her friends. The latter, at least, are replaced by other, more rewarding friendships with women she meets at the community college, but the family losses remain at the end of the book.

Books like this were called "runaway housewife" novels at the time Bryant's book was published, although the women depicted did not actually run away from their responsibilities as wives, mothers, and homemakers. Ella Price and her cohorts were not like Anna Karenina or the wife in *Kramer v. Kramer*. The re-entry women gained some emotional and intellectual independence through their college experiences, however, and this was seen as threatening to their husbands and others, and apparently to the reviewers as well. These women students became more difficult to control as they became more thoughtful, and those formerly in command of their lives feared losing them altogether. Mabel Beasley, Norma Jean's mother in "Shiloh," is a good example of this behavior. She fights for control of her daughter's life in determined and cruel ways, and she blames the community college for her impending loss.

This phenomenon of "punishment" seems to be connected to the resurgence of the feminist movement in the early 1970s. Other examples recur throughout the 1970s and 1980s, but I can find no instances of this kind from the 1990s, nor do I believe that the label "runaway housewife" would be used at present.

The use of "punishment" is reminiscent of the movies of an earlier period where "bad girls" (i.e., those with sexual experience outside of marriage) had to suffer in some way at the end of the story, no matter how heroic or noble their behavior in other areas of life. Sometimes the punishment was death, sometimes just a bullet wound or some lesser penalty; but their daring and presumption in assuming some control of their lives could not go unchecked. And just as the penalty for taking community college classes seems to have died down in the 1990s, the penalty for being sexually experienced has declined as well. Fictional women are still being punished with death, loss and destruction for being "uppity," but the definition of exactly which behavior is too challenging for the powerful to let pass undisciplined has changed. (See *Thelma and Louise*.[9])

Perhaps community colleges are now "off the hook" because the 1990s view of them is so demeaning and attendance has become so ordinary in American life that even housewives no longer threaten anyone when they enroll.[10] On the other hand, the current negative view is more general and includes larger numbers of people. The white, working class re-entry woman remains the standard student character, but she has been joined by others.

There is another recurring pattern in the fiction of the 1970s, this one positive in nature. Attendance at a community college seems to improve the "runaways" by freeing them

---

[9] *Thelma and Louise*, directed by Ridley Scott, 1991, motion picture.

[10] This plot-line has not died out entirely in real life, apparently. In a letter to Ann Landers, the wife of a womanizing alcoholic writes of joining Co-Dependents Anonymous, trying to focus on her own emotional health. "When I declared my independence and enrolled in the local community college, he got the message and insisted I stay home. I refused. When he realized I was serious, he agreed to go with me for counseling, something I had been begging him to do for ten years. Knowledge is power, and that group changed my entire life. [Signed] A New Woman in Florida." Chicago *Tribune*, 4 September 1992, sec. 5, p. 3.

from their heavy dependence on alcohol, in addition to freeing their minds and spirits. An unusual number of them drink too much before their re-entry (or smoke too much or eat too much). Their addictive behavior lessens dramatically after two-year college exposure, or even vanishes entirely. Ella Price is an example. A very conventional thirty-four year old when she first enters college during a period when older students were more unusual than they are today, she becomes more liberal, in step with the Berkeley culture of her era. She marches in an anti-war demonstration, thinks some drugs may be acceptable (although she does not use them herself), and recognizes the existence of gays. Her former drinking and depression diminish, and her self-confidence increases.

I wrote to each author who used a two-year college character, and Dorothy Bryant answered my query at length. She wrote *Ella Price's Journal* in 1968, she says, but it took her four years to find a publisher,

> ... partly because the women's movement needed to get going before publishers saw a market for the book, and partly, I think, because editors were women who had come from upper middle-class backgrounds and had degrees from places like Radcliffe . . . and couldn't relate much to a woman barely on the lower edges of the lower middle-class. It's a class thing.[11] (Dorothy Bryant)

Bryant thinks that the situation has not changed much in the twenty years that followed her novel's publication.

Women's Studies Quarterly in its 1991 Fall/Winter edition asked a dozen prominent feminist academics and writers to give brief accounts of the "Books That Changed Our Lives."[12] The authors one might expect were named—Simone de Beauvoir, Virginia Woolf, W. E. B. DuBois, Tillie Olsen.

---

[11] Dorothy Bryant, unpublished letter to Nancy LaPaglia, 20 November 1991.

But one woman cited Dorothy Bryant, who "conveyed, most convincingly, the struggles of a community college re-entry student to pay attention to her own changes and those of society in the 1960s." This admirer contacted Bryant after reading *Ella Price's Journal,* and they became friends. Her life change due to reading the book came about, she says, "when I realized for the first time that books were written by people, vulnerable people, who feared exposure to critics and yet were brave enough to offer it to us."

There are only three other works from the 1970s with student characters. Since the students are very minor participants, each work is addressed at greater length in the chapter on faculty in fiction.

In Susan Fromberg Schaeffer's *Falling,* there are no scholars in the central character's English class in one of the City Colleges of Chicago.[13] The students are poorly prepared, often silent, and live in a tacky working-class neighborhood. At the end of the semester, they gain some sympathy from their teacher, in contrast to the still negative view she has of the administrators and the other faculty. One student, enormously fat and previously mute, tells her how her life has changed, how she will never forget the class. The teacher herself then modifies her attitude to one of greater sensitivity, if not respect.

In Stephen King's *The Stand,* a minor character, Dayna, has attended a Georgia community college, where she was a jock and was treated poorly by a boyfriend.[14] She becomes a strong and fearless bi-sexual feminist and dies bravely in

---

[12]J. J. Wilson, "Books That Changed Our Lives," *Women's Studies Quarterly* 19, no. 3 & 4 (Fall/Winter 1991): 26-27.

[13]Susan Fromberg Schaeffer, *Falling* (New York: Macmillan, 1973).

[14]Stephen King, *The Stand* (New York: Doubleday, 1990).

Chapter 59 while on a rescue quest. Rather than reveal the name of a fellow spy to the devil, she throws herself out of the top-story window of his headquarters, a Las Vegas hotel.

In the last 1970s novel I found, the students in Dan Wakefield's *Starting Over* are much less dramatic.[15] We see them seated in the central character's communications class, comfortable and mainstream, responding pleasantly to the fumblings of their inexperienced teacher. It is 1970 in a Boston junior college on a nice urban street, and the scene is duplicated in an abbreviated version in the film made of the novel in 1979.[16]

The View From the 1980s

The veil of invisibility lifts a little. Eleven diverse works appear: Bobbie Ann Mason's short story with which I began Chapter 1, four novels, two murder mysteries, a play, a film, a made-for-TV movie, and an episode of "The Wonder Years" that won a Peabody award. The "runaway housewife" contin-ues. Norma Jean Moffitt in "Shiloh" is one of them, as her incipient transformation alienates her mother and frightens the husband who is unable to grow with her.

In K. C. Constantine's murder mystery, *The Man Who Liked Slow Tomatoes*, the white, working-class re-entry woman student who is a major character suffers more than any other "runaway" that I found.[17] She has enrolled in a community college because her husband's unemployment leads to a need to prepare for a job. (This is another common

---

[15]Dan Wakefield, *Starting Over* (New York: Delacorte Press, 1983).

[16]*Starting Over*, directed by Alan J. Pukula, 1979, motion picture.

[17]K. C. Constantine, *The Man Who Liked Slow Tomatoes* (Boston: David R. Godine Publishing, 1982).

pattern, incidentally. "Runaways" often begin college in order to serve their families better, not because of any desire of their own.) She meets a support group whose members contradict every value of her sordid life, a life in which her husband beats her, she has no money or marketable skills, and she is made to feel worthless. However, in the view of her community and of the detective-hero, the support group women are "ladies" who burn their bras and reject femininity. College experience encourages the student to try to correct her own grammar. The author's view of this seems to be that she is deserting her true roots, the authenticity of her Pennsylvania coal mining area, in exchange for unimportant values. Her punishment is great. Her husband is murdered by her father, her father loses his mind, and she commits suicide.

The other murder mystery is Charles Willeford's *Miami Blues*.[18] It is a violent detective story focused on a vicious psychopathic killer who takes up with airhead Susan, a Miami-Dade part-time business major and full-time hooker. She is a poor country girl who came to the big city to work her way through college. The detective-hero, a likeable slob, wonders how anyone as simple-minded as Susan could survive. She outlasts the killer, however, returns to her hometown to marry, and wins a prize for her vinegar pie. In the 1989 movie based on the book, Susan is less of a dope, though still a good cook.[19] She is doing writing assignments for the same English class, and her car has a Miami-Dade Community College decal on the back window. We see it when the killer/boyfriend uses the car in a getaway.

---

[18] Willeford, *Miami Blues*.

[19] *Miami Blues*, directed and produced by Jonathan Demme and Gary Goetzman, 1990, motion picture.

Nancy Pelletier's *The Rearrangement* is another runaway housewife novel, but the runaway this time is on the faculty, so I will discuss it more fully in a later chapter.[20] The students at her community college are seen as products of the open-door policy; they are poorly prepared and ungrammatical. The reader is led to sympathize with them, however, as they try to handle their many other responsibilities and attempt to plan for their futures. The African-American students use wrong verbs, a white student is pregnant, and a friend's daughter at a California junior college is into drugs and failing. Nevertheless, many students are optimistic and hopeful, involved in the "relevant" discussions of the early 1970s.

The last "runaway" that I found avoids most of her "punishment," as this version of the usual story is somewhat softened. In "Pottery Will Get You Nowhere," a 1989 episode of *The Wonder Years*, Mom takes ceramics at the local community college.[21] Her feminist daughter approves, but her husband and two sons do not because she is taking time away from them. Her husband only admires her cooking, not the dish in which it is served. He is jealous when she reports that her male teacher respects her work. He "accidentally" breaks the coffee cup she gave him as a present. Her younger son-narrator describes the family upheaval in geologic metaphors, due to a high school course he is taking at the time. Family changes are like disturbing earth shifts along fault lines. At the end, husband and wife fight, but then they make up lovingly. We hear no more of community college courses for Mom. (At the end of a 1991 episode, in a single-mention, she applies to River Community College in the late 1960s,

---

[20] Pelletier, *The Rearrangement.*

[21] "Pottery Will Get You Nowhere," an episode of "The Wonder Years," January 1989, television series.

after losing her high school secretarial job due to a lack of necessary skills.)[22]

In Dean Corrin's *Butler County*, a play performed at Chicago's Victory Gardens, the student actually gets to run away.[23] She escapes directly from high school, and her punishment is modest. She loses her boyfriend (a very small loss), the uncle who objected to her going to college becomes senile, and her widowed father comes to see the rightness of her decision. The "juco" itself would be a deliverance from Clay Corner, Kansas, but in a semi-happy ending she is helped to a more desired option by a stewardess neighbor new to the area. The central character plans to leave for Wichita State U. with a scholarship and a part-time job. (I was told that the play's director at Victory Gardens got an award from a community college organization for recognizing the existence of the two-year college, but the theater was unable to provide further information and Corrin did not answer my query.)

The central character of T. Glen Coughlin's *The Hero of New York* is one of the rare male students in the literature.[24] Charlie, the nineteen-year-old narrator, hates his Long Island community college. The college and the area are one step up from the Brooklyn working-class neighborhood his family left. He is a bored and failing business administration major, interested only in his waitress girlfriend and the troubles of his policeman father, the hero of the title. On his way to becoming a violent alcoholic like his dad, he is at "Rinky-Dink College," because his father convinced him to stay at

---

[22] "The Wonder Years," 1991.

[23] Dean Corrin, *Butler County*, a play performed at Victory Gardens Theatre, Chicago, 1984.

[24] T. Glen Coughlin, *The Hero of New York* (New York: Norton, 1986).

home instead of leaving for a state university or his fantasized hope, Princeton. Charlie drops out of school and, at the end of the novel, is unsure of his direction. His girlfriend, who left him for a rich dope dealer, is taking a community college course in hair cutting.

The central character in Lee Smith's *Oral History* fares better.[25] She is a student at an Appalachian community college who tapes the history of her "colorful" relatives as an honors project for her English teacher, Dr. Bernie Ripman of Miami. She and her project form a frame around the main body of the novel, which concerns one hundred years of history in Hoot Owl Holler, Kentucky. Her family history is an absorbing weave of folklore, murder, passionate love, and witchcraft. The student's contemporary life is fairly mundane, a more appropriate tone for the minimalist authors who are usually the people who write about white working-class women in community colleges. She and Dr. Ripman (Dr. Rip-off) receive the low-key mocking treatment standard for two-year college inhabitants. She finishes the assignment, however ineptly, and graduates. In the end frame, she elopes with Dr. Ripman, and they move to Chicago.

My discussion of the 1980s will end with two of the more sympathetic portrayals I have located. In Clyde Edgerton's *Raney*, a woman student at Listre Community College in North Carolina marries an assistant librarian at the school, despite their different backgrounds.[26] Librarian Charles Shepherd is more polished and better educated. His family is middle class, and his snobbish mother is disdainful of Raney's backwoods ways. Raney, however, is warmer, more open, and has been able to rise above her racist environment as well.

---

[25] Lee Smith, *Oral History* (New York: Putnam, 1983).

[26] Clyde Edgerton, *Raney* (Chapel Hill, NC: Algonquin Books, 1985).

The description of the couple's relationship can border on sexist drivel, but by the end of the novel they have worked out a peaceable marriage. Charles is the shepherd who realizes he can learn from the child-like candor of his wife, and he too becomes warmer and more open. The community college has little to do with the relationship but remains in the background in a minor role.

Nobody's Child, a made-for-TV movie, is based on the true story of Marie Bartelo, a woman who was wrongly institutionalized for twenty years in a Massachusetts asylum.[27] Perhaps because the story stays close to the facts of the case, it offers a very rare supportive and understanding portrayal of a student, faculty members, and the two-year college itself. Bartelo, called Balter in the film, is played by Marlo Thomas, who hardly imparts the beaten-down image of a loser. Thomas won an Emmy for her performance, and Lee Grant is the woman who directed. (A woman director was a somewhat uncommon choice at the time.)

In the movie, a teacher at a Massachusetts community college helps bring about Balter's release from the asylum, and he and his wife give her a home. Balter succeeds in her studies at his school with the help of a tough but encouraging woman English teacher. She is able to graduate with an A.A. and eventually goes on to acquire a Harvard M.A., a career, and a loving marriage. The marriage is not long-lived, unfortunately, as her husband gets sick and dies. She, clearly a survivor in adversity, will continue on.

---

[27] *Nobody's Child*, 1986, made-for-TV motion picture.

The Contemporary View: The 1990s

Half-way through the third year of this decade, there are already more examples of community college students than in any other decade besides the 1980s, and most of the examples come from television, movies and murder mysteries. (This is true even though the majority of the television leads I received were never followed up.) Thus, they are more widespread, and seen by more people than read the relatively elite novels and *The New Yorker* short stories discussed earlier. Unfortunately, television, even more than literature, is given to stock figures who have stock reactions to stock situations. This does not necessarily make all of them one-faceted losers; nineteenth-century writers like Dickens used stock characters and made many of them memorable and likeable. However, a five-year study of the impact of television on society, which was finished in 1992 by the American Psychological Association, reports that when marginal members of society are portrayed, negative stereotypes are the rule.[28] This finding does not bode well for an increase in positive portrayals of two-year college characters.

The topic of two-year colleges is still obscure, practically imperceptible to the culture at large, but there are four TV programs, two murder mysteries, a movie, a play, and a short story to be examined. They range in their judgement of the two-year college student from laudatory to devastatingly negative. The white, working-class re-entry woman is still with us, but she is no longer the dominating student character.

---

[28] Aletha Huston, et al., *Big World, Small Screen: The Role of Television in American Society* (Lincoln, NE: University of Nebraska Press, 1992). Study done by the American Psychological Association, reported in the Chicago *Tribune*, 26 February 1992, sec. 5, p. 6.

In several entries, she is simply part of a multi-cultural, multi-everything classroom. Maybe our society has grown so used to her, there are so many like her, that she has become a standard part of the scenery.

The four television programs are each episodes in a continuing series. In chronological order of first airing, the episodes are from *The Simpsons*,[29] *Saturday Night Live*,[30] *Night Court*,[31] and *Room for Two*.[32]

Marge, the mother of the Simpson family, renews her interest in art by enrolling in a community college studio art course. She had been a prize-winning high school artist before becoming a homemaker. There are the typical sit-com problems and pratfalls as she attends the course. However, her class work leads to a coveted award. Marge wins a commission to paint Homer's boss, and the community college, along the way, is shown in a nice light.

The community college episode on *Saturday Night Live* so angered some faculty groups that they sent protesting letters to the producers. In the case of *S.N.L.*, it is possible that protests will only encourage them. A skit was performed called "Community College Bowl," a take-off patterned after the college bowls where bright, clean-cut young students vie to answer questions on a variety of academic topics. Here, the usual *Saturday Night Live* crew (male and female, not all white) plays an incredibly stupid bunch who are supposed to be the best the community colleges have to offer. Far from being enrolled in the first two years of the baccalaureate degree, one is majoring in cleaning and minoring in pressing.

[29]"The Simpsons," April 1991, television series.

[30]"Saturday Night Live," 5 October 1991, television series.

[31]"Night Court," Fall 1991, television series.

[32]"Room for Two," 22 April 1992, television series.

They can answer nothing. "Who was the first president of the United States?" They sit mute and deadpan, staring ahead with glazed eyes, chewing gum. No question is easy enough for them.

In an episode of *Night Court* that received a lot of advance publicity, the judge replaces a community college law professor who has been committed to a mental institution, driven insane by his students. The judge himself committed the teacher and later comes to understand how the students accomplished the task. Ed Koch Community College is located on the sixteenth floor of a New York City walk-up. Its mascot is a city pigeon that was caught in an air conditioning vent. The classroom is somewhat battered, there are few supplies, and the class consists of five white men and women of "non-traditional" age, all silly and argumentative. They are there for idiosyncratic and calculating reasons. One is a nerdy, many-penciled fat guy, another is a crook who wants to learn how not to be caught, and a third is a woman who wants to marry a lawyer. The remaining two are a battling older couple who wish to save money with a do-it-yourself divorce. Their attention spans are limited when it comes to a lecture on evidence, but eventually the judge manages to catch the class's interest, and the ending is upbeat.

In *Room for Two*, a widowed mother and her daughter enroll in Psychology 101, a night class of all "non-traditional-aged" students. The mother, new to college, does better on the first exam than the daughter, who already has a college degree. (Enrolling in a two-year college with a four-year degree in hand is not an uncommon pattern today, but this program is the only fictional reference I found to it.) Competitive rivalry results. Then they get the same grade on the second exam, and vow to stop competing. We know they will not. The tone of the program is at least neutral towards the college, the teacher, and the course. In addition, the mother meets a new beau, who is there taking a mime class. Romance and the two-year college system are not often linked.

In *Throw Mama from the Train*, some multi-aged crazies at Valley College in California are trying to become creative writers.[33] The craziest of them, played by Danny DeVito, wants the instructor to murder his ghastly and domineering mother for him. He figures the writing teacher is creative and will therefore be able to commit the crime undetected. The rest of the movie consists of a series of situations in which the instructor tries not to get involved in the crime, and the student tries to get the deed done. There is a happy ending—the mother dies a natural death, the instructor gets a book published based on the crime that did not happen, and several students achieve some measure of success. The now-or-phaned student even publishes a book himself—a children's pop-up book about monsters.

Bill Crider, who wrote *Dead on the Island*, is a community college English teacher in Alvin, Texas, and he uses positive community college mentions or settings often in his murder mysteries.[34] In this book, the missing twenty-year-old daughter of a major character attends a community college in Galveston. She wants to become a lawyer. We meet another young student in the social science department when the detective-hero interviews her a few times. She seems like a normal person. The college itself is shown in a decent light, and the detective corrects the mother when she confuses the community college with a high school. The missing daughter does not come out well. She shows up near the end, involved

[33] *Throw Mama From the Train*, directed and produced by Danny DeVito and Larry Brezner, 1990, motion picture.

[34] Bill Crider, *Dead on the Island* (New York: Walker & Company, 1991).

in her own kidnapping plot and other crimes in order to punish her father.

The other mystery, Edward Mackin's *The Nominative Case*, focuses on faculty rather than students and will be discussed in Chapter 5.[35] Mackin's students generally are poorly-prepared louts involved in a travesty of education in New York City. Sadly, this is one of only two books I found that are actually set entirely in a two-year college. We meet one of the students individually, a suspect in the murder case because he had been threatening the victim for a passing grade. He is a huge, illiterate African-American, stupid and powerful, whose companion is a Latina employee of the college. She is called "a wiry bitch," and she uses his physical strength to further her corrupt plans. The students, the college, and the faculty are treated with utter contempt by the author. Writing under his own name, Ralph McInerney, Mackin is the creator of the Father Dowling series, a very different kind of murder mystery. The Father Dowling books provide a warmly humorous look at the Roman Catholic Church. *The Nominative Case* is a thorough trashing of the urban community college student.

The 1992 version of Trevor Griffiths's 1976 play, *Comedians,*[36] gives an altogether different view of the same group.[37] Griffiths originally set his play in an adult education night school class in Manchester, England. Aaron Freeman, a Chicago writer and stand-up comic, was asked to write additional

---

[35]Mackin, *The Nominative Case.*

[36]Trevor Griffiths, *Comedians* (New York: Grove Press, 1976).

[37]*Comedians,* with additional dialogue and rewriting by Aaron Freeman, performed at Court Theatre, Chicago, April 1992. The identification of the setting as a junior college occurs only in the playbill. The scene listed for Act I and Act III is, "A classroom in a junior college on the south side of Chicago."

and updated material, and he changed the setting to what the
playbill calls "a junior college on the south side of Chicago."
Acts I and III take place in a classroom used by the theater
department. In the original version, all of the students were
English males from working-class and multi-ethnic backgrounds; they have been changed to three African-American
men, two white women, and a Latino. (There is also a future
student who is a Pakistani in both works.) These six students
include a southern "country boy," an angry rapper, two dys-
functional sisters, and two men who will accommodate the
system in order to succeed. The community college houses a
wide variety of people.

Their teacher is the only minority faculty member I have
found. The students come to his class directly from work,
tired, trying to escape from the anonymity of their dead-end
jobs through stand-up comedy. Aching for self-identity and
creative expression, they make jokes about the racial and
ethnic nervousness of their society. The Latino says he's
attending David Duke Community College and taking White
101—Rhythmless Dancing. The rapper stops the show with
a terrifying routine, a piece of performance art about his
encounter with two very white suburbanites who are leaving
the Chicago Stadium after a Bulls game. (The white folks are
blonde-wigged mannequins.) The students are far from ide-
alized or mainstream, but they are smart and often funny, real
people that we might wish well and want to succeed.

Walter Beile's short story, "The Fat Plumber," is the last
work of fiction to be reviewed in this chapter, last for several
reasons.[38] Chronologically, its publication date comes last. In
addition, I prefer to end with a work that is not discouraging

---

[38]Walter Beile, "The Fat Plumber," *The Wright Side* [City Colleges of
Chicago] (April 1992): 12-14.

or depressing. Most importantly, I am the teacher in the story, and Mr. Beile, the author, was my valued student. I urged him to submit his story for publication so that I could include it in my bibliography, and it was accepted by two college magazines. Its audience may not be as wide as that of some fiction, but my study included other works that were published in journals or magazines of limited circulation, and such a rare example of positive outlook could not be ignored.

The student in the story is a white, working-class re-entry man, attending part time. He returned to college later in life than most in order to "fill in the blanks." His mind is charged with ideas, and he thinks seriously about the course readings. Much of the story concerns a conversation with his wife about *The Republic* of Plato and the meaning of education. Both he and his wife were previously widowed before they married, also late in life, and both are interested in learning. We are shown a small window onto a happy second marriage, almost as rare a depiction as an academically sound community college.

"The Fat Plumber" is the only portrayal I found of a student who is past retirement age and is taking college-level courses. In today's two-year colleges, these students are not exceptionally unusual. And, like many re-entry students, they know what they want, they are in college to learn, and they are a joy to their instructors. It is interesting that this very positive picture of the two-year college comes to us from a student who actually knows such a school from the inside.

Summary

1. The typical community college student character is a white, working-class, re-entry woman who is attending part time.

2. Works appearing before the 1970s are rare. The earliest examples concern children of poor immigrants who use the urban junior college as a necessary step on the way to a university degree.

3. The two-year college system is invisible in American fiction for the sixteen years between 1953 and 1969.

4. The 1970s works feature the "runaway housewife," who is "punished" for presuming to attend college. She gains, however, some control of her life, freedom from addictive behavior, and spiritual awakening.

5. The 1980s works are greater in number. The housewife continues, but other types appear, some fairly positive. The most common tone used by the authors towards the students is mockery.

6. There is a shift to mass media portrayals in the 1990s. The white, working-class, re-entry woman is still in evidence, but is no longer the central figure. The range of attitudes towards students is wide, though most often the community college is a setting for comedy.

Chapter 4

Student Journals

> **History is the essence of innumerable biographies.**
> Thomas Carlyle, "On History"[1]

merican fiction seems to reflect only a few facets of reality when it portrays the inhabitants of the two-year college. Where can one look for the rest of the "map?" Academic writers offer more of the same disparaging picture. Many major researchers, all from universities, see little discrepancy between the demeaning fictional image and the "reality" that their research describes. My purpose is not to argue with their findings, nor do I want to follow them with another exposé of the community colleges and their students.

---

[1] Thomas Carlyle, "On History," in *Critical and Miscellaneous Essays* (London: J. Fraser, 1839); quoted in Mihaly Csikszentmihalyi, *Flow: The Psychology of Optimal Experience* (New York: Harper & Row, 1990), 132.

I looked at a body of literature written by those *inside* the system, affected by it and familiar with it, but who have been unheard. By that, I do not mean a defense of the community college by staff apologists who smooth over actual problems and stonewall any criticism, any more than I want an attack by outside writers and researchers looking down at the two-year colleges from further up the hierarchy. As SY1[2] says, "These people see the world from the point of view of a few studying the rest." I wanted to hear from "the rest."

Since this body of literature written by the unheard did not exist, it had to be created. In the fall of 1991 and winter of 1992, forty-seven women who were students and faculty at five community colleges agreed to write journals about their experiences in the system, specifically for my use. Thirty-seven of them actually returned their books to me. These journals constitute another type of literature, autobiographies within a narrowed frame. They were analyzed just as the fiction was, and, in the same way as fiction, they reflect attitudes, opinions, and feelings about the two-year college. In other words, they constitute a composite image from a source other than fiction.

Who were the writers? Here is a general description of the twenty-three students whose journals will be discussed in this chapter. (The fourteen faculty journals will be considered separately in Chapter 6.)

---

[2] Because of an earnest request by several faculty members for anonymity, all journal writers will be identified by code designations only. In addition, several student writers were apprehensive about the accuracy of their spelling. I asked them not to worry about it and assured them that I would not make fools of them by printing every error. Therefore, I have corrected the spelling in some student journals. Also, there was one journal, written by a student for whom English is very much a second language, where I not only corrected the spelling, but changed some of the grammatical construction into more standard English form.

Ten of the thirty-three students who agreed to write a journal for three weeks did not mail the book back to me, for a return rate of 70 percent. This contrasts with a return rate of 100 percent for the faculty journal writers, but it is still quite high when one considers the time-consuming nature of the task and the complex life each writer is juggling. They wrote an average of eight typewritten pages each (after transcription), with a range from four to twenty-eight. In addition, two of the students agreed to be interviewed after the journals were analyzed, so that I might probe into some commonly occurring themes they did not cover originally.

The students attend five different community colleges: Harold Washington College in Chicago, which is urban, and has a large percentage of inner city and/or minority students; Richard J. Daley College, also one of the City Colleges of Chicago, which is largely working-class, with just over half of the population minority; Oakton Community College in DesPlaines, Illinois, which is suburban and more affluent than the others, with a population that is mostly white; Sylvania Campus, Portland Community College in Oregon, located in a medium-size city and mixed in class and background, if not in racial composition; and Mohawk Valley Community College in Utica, New York, located at the edge of an older rust-belt town, with many rural students.

The writers are re-entry students, with one exception; she came to a community college directly from high school. Another writer dropped out of college the semester she kept the journal. The re-entry women became college students via a variety of pathways. Five did not graduate from high school, but passed the G.E.D. test before registering for college-credit courses. Two already have baccalaureate degrees, and one of these two is currently in graduate school. She is picking up undergraduate credits needed for state certification in her field. Three others took some four-year college courses in the past, but perhaps too long ago to fit the definition of the growing category of "reverse transfer student," and two are clearly reverse transfer students.

The phenomenon of reverse transferring is becoming common, and it should be explained at this point. Such students go to the four-year colleges first, even when they may not have the necessary resources to do so. The reasons are many. Going away to a four-year school grants students a cachet among their peers that is irresistible for some, and the reverse of that coin, avoiding the scorn given to those who attend community colleges, is compelling. In any case, these are students who need more academic and financial help than they get. They drop out or flunk out of the four-year college. Once back home, they register at a local two-year college, which gives them more support and is less expensive. Thus, they have transferred, but in reverse order. Often, these students do well at the two-year college and take their credits with them when they return to the "big boys." It is a process very costly in time, pain, and money. It is only better than simply leaving the four-year college as a failure and then *not* registering at a two-year college for a second chance.

Several journal writers reported that when Oregon passed a referendum that increased tuition considerably at state universities, the number of reverse transfers jumped noticeably, and the opprobrium given to those choosing a two-year college lessened at the same time. And the Illinois student who came to the community college directly from a respected suburban high school despite the considerable scoffing of friends and family, reports that, "The funny thing is, at the beginning of every semester, I see more and more students from my high school—the ones that went 'away' to college. It seems that some only find out how good community colleges are after they've been unsuccessful at four-year schools."

A third of the student writers were in their 20s, and the average age was thirty-six, a few years older than the norm in community colleges, but not uncommon when students of "non-traditional" age often outnumber those who are between eighteen and twenty-two. Re-entry students, by their very definition, are going to be older. As I explained in Chapter 1, I chose them because the re-entry woman student was the fictional stereotype, and I wished to hear from her counterpart in the world that I knew.

They were born in fourteen different states, plus Mexico and Poland, a reflection of the great geographic mobility many people have in this country, since the five colleges are located in only three states. Their racial and ethnic makeup is almost identical to the percentages that exist among two-year college students in the United States as a whole, and in their individual colleges as well. Seventeen writers are white (74 percent), three are African-American and three are Latina. There are no writers of Asian background, although I tried to get one or two, but Asians form such a tiny fraction of community college students and faculty that even one would be an over-sampling. The fictional stereotype is white and working-class (as well as re-entry and female), but I wished to see if women with different racial/ethnic or economic backgrounds reported a different experience. Twelve of the twenty-three were married, six single, three divorced, and two separated from their husbands. Five had no children, and the remaining eighteen had from one to ten children, with six of them having two each. The average number of children was about three. At Oakton, the most affluent of the schools, more students were married, and it was more common to have fewer external pressures (mostly of a financial or occupational nature) to go to college. Perhaps not surprisingly, Oakton was the only one of the five colleges to have a 100 percent return rate on the journals from students. Oakton students' lives are filled with juggling responsibilities, just as the others, but they may have more extensive support systems and fewer financial pressures.

Fifteen writers were employed while attending college and fulfilling family responsibilities, with work hours ranging from four to forty-five per week. Their jobs varied from computer programmer to aerobics instructor, to part-time bouncer in a bar, to doing historical restoration. There were four secretaries, two dental assistants and two in health care, an accountant, a child care worker and a home assembler. Eleven of the writers attended college part-time, mostly because of their jobs. This percentage of part-time registration, almost 50 percent, reflects the reality of community college enrollment today in the United States. It is also another characteristic in the fictional stereotype of the community college student. She is a part-time student more often than not.

The students have accumulated an average of forty-three hours of college credit, and their G.P.A. is commonly around a B+\A-. This high G.P.A. is not surprising; those who write readily do better in school, and only those who were willing to write agreed to this study. In addition, re-entry students as a group have a higher G.P.A. than the average.[3] Only two writers are not preparing for a career. One was in college specifically for her "own fulfillment" after raising ten children, and the other, who already had a full-time job and children, was "enrolling in classes for my personal self—

---

[3] J. Conrad Glass and Anita Rose, "Re-entry Women: A Growing and Unique College Population," *NASPA Journal*, 25, no. 2 (Fall 1987): 110-19.

nothing, no one else, only me." All but the last student intend to transfer to a four-year college eventually.

The high percentage of those who say they intend to transfer is not unusual. Most two-year college students say they want to transfer eventually. The number who actually do transfer is considerably lower. The best-documented estimate given today, by Arthur Cohen and his associates at U.C.L.A., is around 13 percent.[4] This percentage does not include students who transfer to private colleges, are reverse transfers or already have degrees, and it *does* include those who never intended to transfer in the first place. The true percentage must be at least a little higher. The rate was estimated at around 25 percent in the early years of this century, when the junior college's principal goal was transfer, so around 15 percent or more seems about right for today.[5] In any case, we cannot predict what percentage of the student journal writers will *actually* transfer to a four-year college; we can state that they do fit the general profile of the two-year college student in that they *say* they intend to transfer in the future.

Six of the writers want a career in business, four in teaching, and four simply give the academic fields in which they hope to transfer—foreign language, women's studies, science and English. The career choices of the others range from social worker to veterinarian to actor to chiropractor. Their socio-economic status may be ascertained to some extent from details given in their journals, and those who are probably at the lower end of the economic scale aim as high

---

[4] Arthur Cohen and Florence Brawer, *The Collegiate Function of Community Colleges* (San Francisco: Jossey-Bass, 1987).

[5] Keith Dobberstein, *The Evolution of the City Colleges of Chicago*, paper given at the Seventh Annual Illinois History Symposium, Springfield, IL, 5 December 1986.

as the others. Often, the community college helps them realize they may reach more ambitious goals than they thought at entry.

> Every class that I successfully complete adds to my confidence. As my confidence grows, I feel better and better about myself and my chances of reaching my goals. (DA7)

> Now I realize I'd like to get a degree and then go on to speech and language or a psychology masters. I figure that by time my girls are going to college I'll be graduated and working in a field that is rewarding to me. There are days when I ask myself if I'm doing the right thing; I no longer doubt I am. I will be forever grateful to my first professor's help and encouragement. (OK3)

The Journals

There are now so many students in community colleges that I have heard people say that the two-year school is the dominant form of higher education in this country today. Whether this is true or not, it is currently the fastest-growing segment of higher education, only in part due to the recession and high unemployment rates. (A recession is always a time of increased enrollment for two-year colleges.) For these reasons alone, what community college inhabitants have to say about their experiences should be worth studying, even if their reports were inarticulate and boring. But they are far from uninteresting, and I found that the journals tell stories that are emotionally moving and rich in metaphor, and give critiques of the two-year college that are valuable for detail and insight.

Four major themes emerged after an analysis. I will call them Agency, Marginality, Joy of Learning, and Juggling. A fifth theme involved the experience of writing the journal itself and appeared less frequently than the others. Perhaps it could be appropriately explored under Joy of Learning, but I wrote about it separately, partly because it surprised and pleased me so much, but mostly because it is only indirectly related to the image of the two-year college. I will address it in Chapter 7 and include at that point the same theme as it appeared in the faculty journals.

Agency

> First you have a topic sentence, she explains to Leroy. Then you divide it up. Your secondary topic has to be connected to your primary topic. To Leroy, this sounds intimidating. I never was any good in English, he says. What are you doing this for, anyhow? She shrugs. It's something to do.[6]
>
> Bobbie Ann Mason, "Shiloh"

Norma Jean Moffitt does not admit to her husband, to her mother, or perhaps even to herself, that attending the local community college is not just "something to do." Her life sort of happens, unplanned. This seeming passivity, this lack of agency, can be found in many of the fictional characters who attend two-year colleges. Norma Jean and her fictional counterparts may go so far as to experiment with choices of action, trying out possible avenues to a different life. For instance, "Shiloh" ends with Norma Jean walking away from her husband, "following a serpentine brick path." But the next step, consciously thinking and planning for the purpose of achieving a goal, does not happen to the fictional characters. What the student journals report is quite different.

---

[6] Mason, *Shiloh and Other Stories*, 11.

The students make plans in order to reach goals. The plans may have been triggered by external events such as divorce or job loss, but these women are deliberate in trying to gain some control of their lives, and they are determined to lead a thoughtful life instead of one that just happens. They do not see themselves as losers or drifters, but as active participants in planning their own futures, even though they may not always succeed. Even those who recount stories of enormous struggle and trauma do not present themselves as victims to be pitied.

Their short-term strategies can be of mind-boggling complexity just in order to get out of the house in the morning, especially for those women with young children. Long-term plans are also complex, but can be concrete, rational, and obtainable as well.

Listen to HW5, a former waitress who raised five children, a "tough cookie" Appalachian who discovered she was a good writer while at the community college. Severe illness led her to think about a job she can manage without standing all day. She is not interested in living on disability payments from the government, and she is only different from the other writers in that she is older than most. Now an honors student, she writes of having to overcome government and City College bureaucracy in order to stay in school and plan for her future. While at the community college, she raised her sights from a certificate in substance abuse counseling to a baccalaureate degree from a prestigious school of social work.

> I kept thinking I was too old to go to school at fifty, but I registered for my G.E.D. test and passed it with flying colors after not going to school for thirty-five years.

I had always been an advocate for the poor and involved with street people, many of them chemical dependent. So I decided to become an alcohol and substance abuse counselor. This last semester was tough. Between diabetes and myasthenia gravis, my two major diseases, full class load, my internship at St. Elizabeth's Hospital in substance abuse and volunteer work full-time in crisis intervention, I had my life all planned out for me. At least life wasn't boring.

And I learned a lot. To my surprise, when final grades came I had five *A*'s and one *B*. I was elated to see that I could do so well. I felt like a pro, a winner of many battles, all within myself. I plan to graduate in December, 1992, and am applying for a scholarship at the Jane Addams School of Social Work at the university. (HW5)

I did not choose to begin with this student because she is any more "colorful" or supportive of my thesis than the others. I chose to begin with this long quotation because it is a good example of a multiple-themed passage. It could as easily have been listed under "Joy of Learning" or "Juggling," or maybe "Marginality." Actually, it could have been under any theme except "Writing the Journal." My assignments as to theme are arbitrary to an extent but are determined at least partly by context. The other quotations given from the journals are usually briefer than the one above, and it must be understood that the choice of theme is best connected to context, even though much of the journal contents will not be seen by the reader.

The journals tell of stress in the life of every writer, but the particular stress that is associated with attending college usually comes from the intentional imposition of a task upon oneself. The pain becomes a price to be paid, but worthwhile in the long run.

When I started investigating career options, I tried to pick a career that would only need a two-year degree, but I realized that those fields would end up being just another job. I decided that going to school would be hard enough. It would take all my determination and dedication, so I better be heading towards my dream. That dream is to teach. (MV2)

I knew I didn't want to work in a factory. Somehow I learned to be strong and teach my daughter to be strong also. My children have to struggle with me so I could come to school, but I think these experiences will make them stronger for their future. (DA9)

OK2: "I knew I needed a career, not just a job." OK7: "I know that I thrive on being more than a secretary." OK1: "I don't know how I will do it, but I will make it. Anything less and I will have cheated myself."

An African-American student with a "take-no-prisoners" method of confronting the world complains of the red tape and incompetent clerks who hinder her progress. She is balancing a full-time job, two children, and a full course load. She says, "To stop would mean what I have worked years to acquire will be lost in a puff of smoke. That alone keeps my mind on the right path to success."

They plan for specific programs or to pass specific courses and are proud when they succeed. They write down the everyday details.

I got a head start on my Organic Chemistry class. I read the chapter on infrared spectroscopy and constructed a chart of the transmittance frequencies of the functional groups. It has already helped a great deal. The instructor asked me the frequency of the hydroxyl group, and I nailed it. (SY3)

I am caught up in all of my classes so I don't have any make-up work to do. I use my spare time to study for business class. This is the class that I spend the least amount of time on, probably because it is not directly related to the field I want. But since my best chance to get into nursing is to have good grades, I'm sure I will be spending more time on this subject. (DA7)

I learned to seek more information as required, and made schedules to allow myself at least 3-4 hours of study time each night. I was able to get my papers all turned in, sometimes ahead of time. I learned not to cram the night before a test. (HW5)

The biggest problem is the uncertainty of not knowing whether you will be chosen to be in the nursing program. Each year about 300 people apply, but only 70 are picked. All your efforts may not even be noticed because of the competition. (DA7)

Even the least articulate of the writers, a woman who spent most of her brief journal scolding the younger students for not being serious about college, impresses the reader as one who is looking for a reflective life, for some control over her fate. It is not easy to find an appropriate quotation from her journal, since she has difficulty in writing directly about herself. She uses the third person plural "women" when she means to express her own feelings. After complaining about cuts in grants-in-aid, she writes:

To me, this is almost like saying the funding offered is being pulled to discourage many adults—mostly women, from returning to re-educate themselves. Funding will always be needed. The American women today need this help. All of the women I have met in the last three years are proud of themselves and are working hard to update their learning. (DA4)

Some organize in their own families when they encounter unanticipated opposition.

> My husband and children were unexpectedly inconvenienced by my returning to school and didn't like it. I was no longer home cooking and cleaning, I was at the library with a study partner. My husband was shocked when I said, "What night would you like to cook dinner?" He finally agreed to give it a try on Saturdays. He and the children are adapting and pitching in more, which is good for them. (OK3)

This came from the journal of a woman who is now planning to get an M.A. in psychology and no longer doubts her ability to do so. She is very much like Mom in "The Wonder Years" episode in Chapter 3—an attractive blonde with three children, taking only one or two courses at a time. Comfortably mainstream, she is as apple pie and Mrs. America as anyone could imagine. But what different endings to their stories! Mom in "The Wonder Years" gives up in the face of opposition, even with the support of her feminist daughter. OK3 has plans for herself *and* her family and finds the strength to take them with her.

Her story and that of three others are in the only journals that tell of family opposition to their being in college, opposition ranging in seriousness from children grumpy about going to a babysitter to a husband who says she is "very bitchy" and wonders if the marriage can survive another semester. The nineteen other writers tell of supportive husbands, children, parents, and siblings. I understand that I may not be getting the whole story about their family relationships, but I do not assume that the positive incidents that are recounted in the journals are lies.

In upstate New York, where the recession is severe and of long standing, couples make plans together in order to safeguard future security.

My husband is working two jobs. It's really hard on him, but he knows how important going to school is for me. (MV5)

My husband usually finishes the cooking or does it entirely. Without his support and the network of kid-care that we've established, I would find it impossible to pursue my associates of science degree. (MVX)

In fiction, as we saw, family opposition is common; the percentages of support or hindrance found in the journals is reversed, especially in relation to husbands. Much of the drama in fiction about two-year colleges comes from conflict with those close to the re-entry student. Much of the drama in *all* fiction comes from conflict.

It is also true that all of the husbands in the journals are *1990s* husbands, and the worst examples of family resistance come from the fiction of the 1970s and 1980s. Therefore, at least part of the difference between fiction and the journals might come from the fact that we may be looking at snapshots taken ten or twenty years apart. The intentional commitment to achievement that the journals report may be easier today, when we find statements like that of OK9: "The more I learn, the more he [her husband] loves it." Or DA7: "My husband is a big help with the kids. He watches the little ones while I'm at school, and he supports what I want to do." No fictional character says anything even remotely like this.

Marginality

> Norma Jean works at the Rexall drugstore, and she has
> acquired an amazing amount of information about
> cosmetics. . . . At Christmas, Leroy bought an electric organ
> for Norma Jean. She used to play the piano when she was in
> high school. "It don't leave you," she told him once.
>
> Bobbie Ann Mason, "Shiloh"[7]

People can reveal the fact that they are marginal, on the fringes of the power centers of their society, in the way that they describe their lives or by the way they are depicted by others. They can take a further and more reflective step by demonstrating that they are *aware* of their own marginality; they can articulate their feelings and thoughts about their status. A possible third step is not only an individual process, but a group process or a community process. That is, in addition to personal transformation, people can organize within society in order to tackle injustice to bring power to the marginalized. All three of these aspects of the theme of "Marginality" appear in the student journals.

Frequently, the students discuss socio-cultural aspects of their lives that can be seen as marginal. Most of them are struggling financially, all are women attending low-status schools, some are raising children by themselves, two are physically disabled, six belong to racial or ethnic minorities, one identifies herself as an incest survivor, several are on public aid, one is a lesbian, five are high school drop-outs, and several others had to take remedial classes before they were allowed to register for college-credit courses.

With two exceptions, they do not write English as un-grammatically as Norma Jean speaks. They do not devote

---

[7] Ibid., 2.

their journals to the minutiae by which we know low-status people in fiction—the fast food they eat, the supermarket brands they buy, the mass market entertainment they consume. Housework and child care are presented in the journals as the political issues they actually are. Many describe, in abundant detail, exactly what is involved in getting out of the house in the morning in order to get to their first class. Other topics are usually covered in broader strokes, but whatever the theme, the overall tone of each journal is almost always serious and thoughtful.

In the theme of "Marginality," I am most interested in their awareness of their situation, their consciousness that a hierarchical society is trying to keep them at the edges. We will see in Chapter 6 that the faculty are acutely aware of this phenomenon, and we saw in the previous chapter that very few fictional characters have even a clue that the issue exists.

Many students are aware of their marginality as women.

It really bugs me when I offer input and I give alternatives, and men get so put off. Generally speaking, women I know fight for what they believe in, men acquiesce to women and then talk bad about them behind their backs. It bothers me. This college was not and is not set up for women to learn about women, about life without a hierarchy. (SY1)

Several of my school mates talk about two science instructors who feel it is their duty to espouse their belief that young mothers do not belong in school; they belong at home, tending their babies and not books, cooking dinner, not cultivating their minds. They both point this out at every available opportunity. The women feel they are singled out for public embarrassment. (SY6)

Or they are marginalized for political opinions, such as being against the Gulf War. Says a young vet,

> Though I really could use the money, I feel so relieved
> not to be getting my Army money now. I feared walking
> past the veterans' office wearing a pro-anything shirt—
> fearful they would catch me and take away the money I
> earned after three years in my private war. (SY1)

Others are marginalized for their ethnic backgrounds. One
Latina, a reverse transfer student, felt she was treated poorly
at the small liberal arts college she first attended. She finds
the community college "a different world—friendly and
welcoming. But now I find it hard to believe I am not stupid."

All the student writers but one are aware that the college
where they are registered, at great personal cost and effort, is
demeaned by the larger culture. Attending a two-year college
is not seen by the outside world as a dignified thing to do with
one's life. Several schools have pejorative nicknames. Oakton
is "Joketon," Daley is "Ford City U.," in reference to a nearby
shopping mall. When I asked some faculty in Oregon about
nicknames, they replied, "PCC [Portland Community Col-
lege] *is* pejorative in our area." Younger students do not admit
to their former high school classmates that PCC is where they
are headed. Each of the colleges reported similar stories of
denial. One writer reports,

> When I used to dream about going to college, one thing
> I really wanted was a sticker in my window with my
> school name. To me that meant I was special, smart and
> that I fit in. I have to admit, the comments I've gotten
> from outsiders since coming to MVCC have made me
> ashamed to put the decal on my car. (MV2)

Older students acknowledge their attendance at the community college to neighbors and friends, but learn to expect
the put-down in response, however oblique or genteel. OK1:
"That's a baby college." OK6: "That's the place of last resort."
MV2: "It's the high school after high school." OK6: "A

community college is *preparation* for college." The students themselves joke about the attitudes they face. OK8: "Hey, for 20 bucks a credit I can suffer through a community college. No one will have to know I go there, and all I need to do is pass." They endure the cracks and the sideways glances, and they sometimes fight back.

> My instructor made the most outrageous remarks that led me to believe he is elitist. I wondered if he would dare to say them if he weren't teaching a class that was predominantly minority and female. I finally got up the nerve to politely challenge him when he said people in my profession were dumb as dishwater. (HW10)

Another woman, who is seen as a source of information by her friends and neighbors, says, "I wonder if they ever take into consideration that I have acquired this knowledge from a community college system." Later, angry at the negative media, she gives voice to that question. "I *know* the people they're putting down. People who hold two and three jobs to keep in school, who work hard and pay for everything they get. Struggle and do *well*."

"I *know*"—that is the essential difference between the journal writers and the outside world. They *know* otherwise. Some writers admit to sharing the negative opinions previous to enrolling and then changing after actual experience opened their minds. Some have even found a haven in the two-year college.

> Many times in our daily surroundings we are taken for granted. . . . Even at our workplace we are sometimes, most times, expected to do things that are considered womanly things—basically clerical functions because of our sex. School then becomes a place where we are appreciated for our minds. It is a place where we can be and are treated as equals, regardless of sex. (HW8)

DA7: "The c.c. provides an atmosphere which every person can fit into, and they are the only place where *everyone* really gets a chance to get an education." OK2: "My confidence was at basement level, but this was the best thing that ever happened to me. I recommend the community college to anyone at any age."

> A c.c. teacher told me that life is a collection of stepping stones and you make it to the end one step at a time. So I don't listen to the dream stealers who want to snatch my dreams away and say I can't. (OK1)

This "step" metaphor for the two-year college appears many times. OK1: "No matter what your past or what the future holds, the c.c. is here, a step waiting to be taken and each step one closer to your goals." DA9: "The community college is the first step up for women who are down—the only step available. And taking it is teaching my kids something, also." MV2: "I am proud of my marks. I'm proud of how nice this campus is and I'm proud to be a college student. This was the right step for me."

The "step" they refer to is often the step away from poor self-esteem. Over and over, the two-year college helps them to value themselves. (I will discuss the issue of self-esteem further under "Joy of Learning.")

Of twenty-three writers, twenty-two bring up the marginality of the two-year college system unbidden and share their anger at its unfair image. This is amazing when we remember that their journals were totally open-ended in subject matter as well as in format. (The only direction given was, "Write about your experiences in the two-year college.") We will see later in Chapter 6 that the faculty are stronger yet in their outrage at the injustice heaped upon their students.

Who was the exception that seemed unaware of marginality? A Mexican-American student in her thirties, who immigrated as a ten-year-old orphan, was raised by an older sister, and never dreamed she could even graduate from high school. She is raising four kids by herself and struggling through college so that she can support them better, and for her own growth as well. (I *love* these women! How can anyone treat them as losers and clowns, when they need all the support they can get?) In her journal she never showed an awareness of marginality of any kind, so I chose her as one of the two students who was interviewed so that I could probe for a missing theme with direct questions.

The interview took place in a noisy corner restaurant in an old working-class neighborhood, jackhammers tearing up the dusty street outside. She showed up dressed and coiffed appropriately for a mid-management position, a future goal of hers, I think. She looked great and was justifiably proud of herself. She said she didn't realize that there was discrimination in our culture, or that she was even a minority, until she was older. "Why am I a minority? I'm not inferior." Her son, a freshman in high school, brought the low status of her college to her attention just recently. His teacher told the class to "work hard so you don't wind up at a community college." "My *mother* goes to a community college," he said, and the teacher gave what might be taken for an apology. The mother was surprised at his story, but proud of him for speaking up.

I can remember only two other occasions in my life when I encountered surprise from a student at hearing that the community college has low status. Both of the people involved were African-Americans from the inner city. A two-year college looked like "up" to them. Perhaps the Mexican-American student felt the same way.

Several writers went further than perceiving the marginality and expressing their anger at its unfairness. They organized.

I am on a committee to get a Women's Studies Department established. Of course it will take time and planning
to be recognized but we are persistent. We will overcome
the silence of women. (HW5)

I am talking about organizing a sitter exchange for those
of us with young kids. You know, where you sit for each
other instead of paying money. We women need that help,
and can help ourselves. (DA9)

The first thing on the agenda is to lobby for Women's
Studies. I find myself wavering, though. Those voices,
"What do you expect?" As if science programs are more
important, as if history is more important, than women's
stories. I have to remember this. I have as much right to
those two years as other people do. (SY1)

A young student in Illinois, a woman who was sexually
abused for many years as a child, is now an organizer and
officer of a women's group at her college. A student in Oregon
admires another woman who is assertive in developing study
groups among the math students. She benefits from the
groups, and adds that, "It is hard to validate one's view or
feelings in isolation."

I am convinced that this wish or desire to be part of a
cooperative movement, in a group project that can help others
and themselves, is a major factor in the phenomenon of total
strangers agreeing to add yet another ball to their juggling act
and write a journal for three weeks so that I could complete
my work. I will discuss this circumstance further in Chapter
7.

The most politicized of the student journal writers questions everything—the government, foreign policy, sexism,
racism, Third World poverty, you name it. She is a leader in
two consciousness-raising and protest groups, one a feminist
women's union. She heads the other group.

I am now the new facilitator for the gay and lesbian group because I kept questioning the actions of the guy who was previously the facilitator. He was stuck in the hierarchy and he was making decisions about funds, direction and what not without consulting the group. So I called him on it and said, "Look, I don't care if only one person voices a differing opinion, it is a voice that needs to be heard," and that he needed to ask what people think about the group. The next day he resigned his position. I felt bad, but someone had to say something. (SY1)

She is in the process of coming out, slowly and cautiously, while she writes her journal, and her last entry recounts her anxiety and excitement about a large open meeting she has organized and is to chair the next morning. It was very hard for me not to telephone her after I finished reading, to say, "How did it go?" At the end of reading many of the journals, I wanted to call the writers and ask, "And *then* what happened?" but I decided to stay out of their lives, at least until I have completed the book that they have asked to read.

The Joy of Learning

> "I never raised no daughter of mine to talk that-a-way,"
> Mabel says. "You ain't seen nothing yet," says Norma Jean.
> She starts putting away boxes and cans, slamming cabinet
> doors.
>
> Bobbie Ann Mason, "Shiloh"[8]

All of the students comment on the joy of learning in some way, as does every teacher except one. (Thus, she became the one faculty member I interviewed after the journals were read and analyzed.) Many students also wrote about

---

[8] Ibid., 12.

the *lack* of joy endured during some "learning" experiences, and I will discuss those entries as well. The sense of joy or its absence that involves specific encounters with faculty will be left for Chapter 6, which focuses on the faculty journals.

"The Joy of Learning," as I am using the theme here, refers to individual experiences and not the joint ventures discussed under "Marginality," where critical consciousness led to group action and brought its own kind of pleasure. A student writing about personal experience may describe joy in an event that lightened a day, or in more transformational terms, a learning experience that is long-lasting and signifi- cant. The latter is a metamorphosis, not in the traditional myth of becoming more physically beautiful that is promoted by our advertising and our fairy tales, but a blossoming of mind and spirit, a maturing into independent adulthood. And, again unlike the ads and fairy tales, the prize won is not romance with a rescuing prince but one's own life.[9]

I would like to begin with a kind of experience that journal after journal recounts. It might more properly be called "The Joy of Learning I Am Intelligent." All but one writer mentions, at least in passing, low self-esteem in her past or present. Many say they entered the two-year college with low self-esteem. Or, while at the college, other aspects of their lives reinforce low self-esteem. (Note: No writer says that her experiences with the two-year college made her feel *worse* about herself.) Most are struggling with a learned inferiority, perhaps an aspect of their marginality, but they refuse to allow it to be fixed permanently in their psyches.

---

[9] Three writers did mention romance, however. The episodes ranged from an attraction to a lab assistant, to a liaison with a younger fellow student, to a satisfying marriage to a young man met on campus for whom she plays *You're My Soul and Inspiration* on the jukebox.

I must accept the idea that just maybe I am smart, and that is scary. So many people for so long have made me feel stupid, that the choice is difficult to make. (HW8)

They rejoice in each badge of worth that the community college brings. DA9: "I'm very proud to say that in my second semester I was on the Dean's list. For the first time in my life I have received Honor." OK2: "What a thrill to get an *A* on a test." DA8: "When I returned to class after an illness, I was treated like Queen for a Day by everyone."

I just got off the phone with my English professor, and found out the grades for my last two essays. I had to hold back screaming on the phone, I was so happy. I worked really hard and it paid off. How gratifying! (MV5)

Many of the students tell how they share their joy with their families.

I am the first child in a family of 6 to go to college, so my family is rooting for me 100%! I call them often with test grades and general progress reports. I love to hear the "great job" and screams of excitement on the other end of the phone. (MV5)

My children are proud of me because I returned to school. Let me tell you that learning to adjust to a new way of life is not easy, but it is a very positive change. I learned to communicate to my children so they could understand me better. (DA9)

This is the best decision I ever made, because of the new relationship with my husband. I had confidence that I was a good mother and wife and lover, but I thought that I could never keep up with him in intelligence. That has now changed. (OK9)

Many writers now see themselves in a different light after experience at the two-year college.

My confidence was at basement level after a painful divorce. Has college ever changed that. I found out how smart I was. People liked me and enjoyed my company. I am no longer a doormat for anyone. (OK2)

It took me a year and a half of taking one course a semester to gain the confidence to take more. The more I took, the better I liked it. I discovered something else. I love to learn. (OK9)

I never thought of myself as having anything good to share about my life. Since all my life was very harsh, I learned to survive in this world the hard way. My speech class opened a whole new way of thinking. I learned to talk to people and to let myself go. My life is getting richer every semester because now I have something to look forward to. College is a beautiful experience. (DA9)

Specific concrete situations can bring pleasure. DA9: "I was excited to use a computer for the first time." OK9: "This was my favorite semester—listening to the beautiful words and phrases of Shakespeare and then going on to listen to Bach and Mozart. What an exhilarating day!"

The community college is often a haven to those whose lives are filled with stress.

The satisfaction and feeling of growth (personal) is what makes it all worth while. In days like these it has been extremely important and *necessary* so that I may not lose myself in the insanity of the problems surrounding me! (HW8)

I have been a "hider" educationally, but smaller class-rooms and instructors who are not publishing gave me the boost I imagined. It's not been fun to get a grade of *F* in motherhood from my teen-age daughters, and I needed self-esteem. At times, due to self-destructive teenage difficulties my daughter was experiencing, classes at the community college became a reinforcement for my self-esteem. (SY9)

Of course, two-year college experience is not all joyful, and students also write about these episodes.

There were times I was under so much stress I couldn't deal with it. Watching a film about stress, I started crying very softly within myself. I controlled myself not to do anything foolish, but after class I was just worn out. (DA9)

It is most discomforting if I think I will receive anything other than an *A*. I once bought a funny card for someone which had a stiff cartoon character lying in bed with a stricken look on his face. "Rude Awakening #47." Inside, the card read, "Nobody really cares what your GPA was." I never sent the card. Somehow it seemed more appropriate for myself. (SY7)

Will I ever take another class at a junior college? I don't really know, but probably not. I'd rather study on my own or pick up my knowledge in workshops. (HW10)

SY8: "My life has been in constant turmoil the past few months." HW3: "There is always the thought of dropping out drifting through my mind, but I find the strength to keep on going."

However, the overall impression of the journals is this: An expression of growth, of change for the better. DA9: "My life will never be the same as it was before I started school." MV5: "Going to college is the best thing I could have done!" MV2: "I want to know it all."

The people I've met have touched my life and have caused me to grow and think. I know that I am a better person for having met them. I plan to take classes as long as I can. I never want to stop learning. The value can't be counted in dollars or cents; it is something that can never be taken from you. (SY4)

What I thought was the worst decision I had ever made turned out to be the best choice for a lifetime. At the beginning, I thought the community college would take away all my options. Instead, it was the road toward wonderful opportunities. (OK6)

Juggling

> Leroy remembers to drink from his Coke. Then he says, "You and me could start all over again. Right back at the beginning." "We *have* started all over again," says Norma Jean. "And this is how it turned out." "Is this one of those women's lib things?" Leroy asks. "Don't be funny," [says Norma Jean].
>
> Bobbie Ann Mason, "Shiloh"[10]

The following extended metaphor from one of the student journals is a good way to describe the lives these women juggle. The section on this theme will be brief, not because it doesn't take up a large part of every journal, but because it is usually phrased in mundane detail after detail after detail. In addition, many of the quotations in previous sections will have already given the reader an idea of the complex time management required of these students and of the stress it brings.

School is going great, if impending avalanches are great. It always goes this way—this first week the instructors lob a snowball at us. Some get the snow right in the face and drop the class. The rest of us duck or dodge and the snowball misses us, only to start an avalanche behind us

---

[10]Mason, *Shiloh and Other Stories*, 15.

that we spend the remainder of the term trying to keep ahead of. Sometimes you can feel the snow in your shoes and are certain that you are about to be overwhelmed. I know a few students who seem to surf the avalanche, thriving on the thrill. I just try not to look over my shoulder much. (SY3)

The intentions of the students are conscious. A student with a particularly complicated schedule is ambitious, but says, "Dreams are built on our goals, and goals are built on our values. I value my family highly, so I'll alter my plans for the time being." DA9: "I learned to take one semester at a time so I won't get so overwhelmed and discouraged."

> What I would like to do is quit my secretarial job and go back to school full-time in the fall. I would have to get an evening job waiting tables to pay the rent, and hopefully I could get some financial aid. (SY8)

> I quit my job and found a part-time job as a dental assistant. I have taken an $11,000 a year cut in pay. Financially, it's very hard in my home. I'm thinking of taking another part-time job. If I do, however, I'm afraid I won't have enough time for school, work, studying and homework. (MV2)

Many situations occur that were not predicted or predictable. The juggling may become impossible.

> The past two weeks have been full of S-T-R-E-S-S. Deadlines for some major papers couldn't have been planned for a worse time!!! I have also come to realize how I took preparing for holidays for granted. All of a sudden I was overwhelmed by the prospect of hosting fifteen for Thanksgiving dinner and preparing three comprehensive papers, plus three abstracts and two speeches. (OK7)

After a long frustrating day at work, the last thing I want
to do is go to my calculus class and then have to deal with
the homework. It seems as though I always do things the
hard way and figure things out later in life than most
people. (SY8)

Our daughter tried to commit suicide. It was very difficult
to sit through classes in such a state. How can I pretend
to be normal and friendly to others? (SY7)

SY3: "New wrinkle in my plans for my education. I might be
pregnant." OK8: "Sick kids. Sick husband. It's amazing I'm
healthy. I am in class because my husband felt I needed a
break from taking care of everyone."

Sometimes the two-year college system may not help the
student cope with stress and juggling. The most complaints,
by far, were lodged against the two Chicago schools. And they
are, predictably, the colleges with most of the minority writers. This doubles the burden of the already marginalized
minority women. As Gary Orfield and his colleagues wrote
in their studies of the Chicago public school system, including
the community colleges, the very students who need the *most*
help in order to succeed in college get the least.[11] The most
common faults mentioned were that the bureaucracy is too
big and uncaring and the counselors either lack knowledge or
are unavailable.

The three other colleges are not without problems. Financial worries head the list.

Maybe I'm spending too much time talking about finances, but I tell you, finances are on everyone's mind
here. Financial aid is like a maze of tricks that only a few

---

[11]Gary Orfield, *Toward a Strategy of Urban Integration: Lessons in School
and Housing Policy from Twelve Cities: A Report to the Ford Foundation* (New
York: Ford Foundation, 1981).

have a map to, and they won't say anything. But, hey, that's bureaucracy. (SY1)

I learned that I could not handle a full load, but being on Public Aid, I'm forced to be a full-time student. I had to learn to juggle through my semester. I got what I wanted—three classes for balance, and Public Aid got what they asked for—gym and counseling to make me a full-time student. (DA9)

At other times, the two-year college system gives students the support they need in order to succeed.

My son goes to pre-school here while I study and attend one class. The Early Childhood Center is for me without a question of a doubt the most valuable resource the college has to offer. Its philosophy provides an environment of encouragement, and constructively directs the children in activities. (OK8)

DA7: "Without the scholarship I would not be able to afford to come to school full time." OK8: "As a busy mom, media-based courses offer me the flexibility to study when I want to and go at my own pace. This benefits everyone, especially my family."

And help can come from a stranger, unexpectedly, pleasantly, when a boost is needed.

I remember being helped by the comments of a fellow history student whose children were grown. She attended school full time. When I inquired if she had much time for cooking (I was taking fewer credits and didn't make traditional dinners regularly), she stated that she and her husband ate from the deli. Sometimes it's nice to know that everyone else is not "super woman." (SY7)

Summary

1. The student writers take an active part in planning their lives. They are not passive, waiting for life to happen, but are goal-oriented and reflective.

2. The students recognize their marginal status and resent it. Many organize in an attempt to correct unfair treatment. They are serious and thoughtful people. The negative image of the community college system is improving in some areas due to the reverse transfer phenomenon.

3. The students take joy in learning, especially in learning they are intelligent. They see themselves as maturing into independent adulthood, and they are proud of their successes. Generally, their families are also proud of them, and they write of more family or spousal support than opposition.

4. They use complex strategies to accomplish their goals. There is much stress in every life, but students at the wealthiest school seem to have fewer external pressures and may be able to complete tasks more easily.

5. The community college is a haven for many students. It helps them raise their self-esteem and it is seen as a step in the right direction. Instances of growth and change for the better occur frequently.

6. There are complaints, especially about the large urban system, of hindering bureaucracies and poor counseling. However, in addition to the help that comes from excellent teachers (discussed in Chapter 6), services are sometimes provided that increase the possibility of success.

Chapter 5

Two-Year College Faculty in Fiction

> Before I cease mapping the desert [of the universities], I
> must include some oases . . . [T]here are community colleges,
> where thousands of able and intelligent men and women
> take their teaching opportunities with the greatest
> seriousness and give more than value received. These
> institutions, with close ties to their parent communities, free
> for the most part of the snobbish pursuit of the latest
> academic fads that so warp their university counterparts,
> and free also of the unremitting pressure to publish or
> perish, are, I believe, the hope of higher education in
> America.
>
> Page Smith, *Killing the Spirit: Higher Education in America*[1]

Very little in American fiction corroborates Professor Smith's judgement. He himself mentions the community college just once again in his book, which may be considered a kind of compliment, given his thesis. Community colleges, he writes, are not "killing the spirit" of students

---

[1] Page Smith, *Killing the Spirit: Higher Education in America* (New York: Penguin Books, 1990), 19.

by slavish devotion to research and the ambitions of professors.

These teachers, praised by Smith, are little noticed in our
culture. After several years of intensive searching, I have
found only thirty fictional works that have community college
faculty in them, not counting the single-mentions that I wrote
about in Chapter 2. They include characters in twelve novels,
six television programs, three movies, three short stories,
three murder mysteries, a children's book, and a play. There
is also the third-person autobiography I wrote about earlier.

All but one of the faculty members are white, three-
fourths are male, and two-thirds are in the English Department. So a white male English teacher is the norm for
community college faculty in fiction. Greater variety is found
in their geographic locations, since they work in thirteen
different states and in various sections of the country. Few
could be described as the competent or dedicated teachers
Smith celebrates. I will discuss them in rank order as determined by my analysis of their competence.

Good Teachers

The dedicated few can be very good, indeed. In *Nobody's
Child*, a made-for-TV movie, Marlo Thomas portrays Marie
Balter, who was wrongly institutionalized for twenty years in
a Massachusetts asylum.[2] A community college teacher and
his wife rescue her and give her a home. She then finds an
academic home in a community college English class with a
strict but supportive woman teacher. After extensive faculty
help, she eventually goes on to earn a Harvard M.A. and

---

[2] *Nobody's Child*, 1986, made-for-TV motion picture.

establish a satisfying marriage. In an especially rare depiction, the college itself is portrayed as a place where something as valuable as this could conceivably take place. As I mentioned earlier, the fact that this story is based on a true-life situation may be one reason that it is unusually positive in tone.

In the revised Chicago version of the English play *Comedians* by Trevor Griffiths,[3] the setting has been changed from a Manchester night school to one of the City Colleges of Chicago.[4] The theater arts teacher is now an African-American man who is wise, committed, and kindly. He plugs away semester after semester, managing to maintain his enthusiasm despite setbacks and disappointments. He is empathetic with his multi-cultural, multi-aged students, but tries to uphold moral standards for them at the same time. "A joke that feeds on ignorance starves its audience," he tells one student after a hate-filled routine. This teacher is the only minority faculty member I have found.

Near the end of the novel *The Rearrangement* by Nancy Pelletier, the central character becomes an Ohio community college English teacher, after a rocky time as a re-entry student at a four-year college and graduate school at a university.[5] On the way, she loses her abusive husband to divorce and her beloved youngest son to a car accident, but she finds herself in the process and establishes her independence as a teacher. She has curbed her excessive drinking and has given up the peace-at-all-costs buffer role she has played all her life. The community college itself is marred by the rigid and piggish behavior of some male administrators and faculty, but she and a few of the other women on the faculty are dedicated

---

[3] Trevor Griffiths, *Comedians* (1976).

[4] *Comedians*, revised by Aaron Freeman (1992).

[5] Pelletier, *The Rearrangement*.

and attempt to teach well. Although she deems her college as, "No hall of ivy," and her students use incorrect verbs, get pregnant, and exhibit other "non-collegiate" behavior, she has learned to accept them and herself by the end of a respectable first semester.

In *The Fat Plumber*, a short story printed in a college literary magazine, an older male student praises his Humanities teacher.[6] "She swings into the room every morning with a lot of energy, her eyes sparkling as though she can't wait to get started." She likes her job, he believes, because of her high regard for education. She introduces him to *The Republic* of Plato, which leads him to some serious thoughts about the meaning of society. He is happily married, and much of the story consists of a conversation with his wife about the class, his teacher, and what the ideal education might be.

In Jade Snow Wong's *Fifth Chinese Daughter*, the faculty of the recently opened San Francisco Junior College in 1939 are attentive to the young Chinese-American's needs and open up new worlds of thought and skill to her.[7] She turns to them for advice and support in her bid to transfer to a university. They write ardent letters of recommendation for her. She is excited to be the commencement speaker at her graduation, where she praises the values she has found at the junior college, values that address with respect her two cultures—Chinese and American.

That's about it for the good guys. Glen Bateman, a major character in Stephen King's *The Stand*, was a sociology teacher at a Vermont community college before a killer virus eliminated almost the entire population of the world, but we meet him after the wipe-out, and anyway he didn't like it at

---

[6] Beile, "The Fat Plumber," 12-14.

[7] Wong, *Fifth Chinese Daughter*.

the college and they didn't like him.[8] He is happy to spend his time, now that his colleagues and students are all dead, as a bad amateur painter. Witty and talkative, he serves as the social theorist for a few survivors as they try to re-establish society in Boulder, Colorado. He is treated by the others, who are mostly working-class "man-of-the-people" types, as an academic with some status, especially once they discover he is not a "sissy." He dies heroically near the end of this 1,141-page book, still talking and theorizing, serving as a patriotic spy in the devil's lair.

OK Teachers

Some two-year college teachers are at least OK. The central character of *Starting Over* is a PR man, an alcoholic womanizer during most of his life, but when we see him teaching communications at a Boston community college for a brief time, he is not bad.[9] He does not think his students are dumb, he treats them seriously, and he doesn't sleep with the women. He thinks teaching may be the best thing in his life. At the end of the novel, however, he will be leaving for a new PR firm and more money, a decision made by his Steel Magnolia bride. In the film of *Starting Over*, much has been changed from the book, but a scene depicting the first class he teaches remains.[10] Nervously beginning to teach creative writing and thinking he has prepared for an hour's worth or more, he dismisses the class when he is finished with his material. He looks at his watch, and finds out that only four

---

[8] King, *The Stand*.

[9] Wakefield, *Starting Over*.

[10] *Starting Over*, 1979, motion picture.

minutes have passed. His students, mostly white and main-stream, are pleasant and clean-cut, and the school is located on a nice urban street in downtown Boston.

In a *Room for Two* episode, a male Psychology 101 teacher, a secondary character seen briefly, is OK, also.[11] The tone of the program is at least neutral towards the teacher, the course, and the community college.

The central character in *Falling*, Susan Fromberg Schaeffer's fine first novel, begins her teaching career at one of the City Colleges of Chicago.[12] Elizabeth is in much-needed therapy and takes the job temporarily, along the way to getting well. Although she despises the school, the neigh-borhood, most of the other faculty, and the low level of student preparation, she is an OK teacher. Maybe more than OK. Her students improve in their writing skills and in critical think-ing. When a student who had been silent all semester tells her how much Elizabeth has changed her life, she realizes she had been *pretending* she was not really teaching and that the students meant nothing to her. She will be sorry to leave the job for a four-year school, although she never thinks seriously about staying.

The judge in the television series *Night Court* teaches a law class as a substitute teacher at Ed Koch Community College.[13] He is replacing a man who has been institutional-ized, driven crazy by the students and the job. The episode and the characters are farcical, but eventually the judge catches the interest of the class by what could be called good teaching. His lecture on evidence is ineffective, but then he does a magic trick. He "loses" a coin, plants it in a student's

---

[11]"Room for Two," 1992, television episode.

[12]Schaeffer, *Falling*.

[13]"Night Court," 1991, television episode.

purse, and then "finds" it. The students become interested in discussing the legal question, and the episode has an upbeat ending.

Might-Be-OK-If-We-Knew-More-About-Them Teachers

In *Space Station Seventh Grade*, a children's book, the central character's stepfather teaches English at the local community college, but the book is centered on the relationship between the boy and his family, and we learn little about classroom performance.[14] No particular feeling about the community college is depicted, but the stepfather seems nice enough, a tolerable guy with some fairly harmless quirks.

The central female character in the movie *Bull Durham* is a part-time English teacher in North Carolina who has sex with a different baseball player each season.[15] She is knowledgeable about the game and helps their performance on the field as well as in bed. She is an incense-burning New Ager, sort of a late 1960s previous-and-future-lives type reminiscent of Shirley MacLaine. She quotes academically respectable poets like Blake, Whitman, and Dickinson, however, so she may have some knowledge of her field. And she may be as caring and helpful a teacher in the community college as she is in the ball park. We never see that part of her life.

The Women's Room, Marilyn French's 1977 best-seller, begins and ends with the central character teaching at a small Maine community college, which she sees as a discouraging

---

[14]Jerry Spinelli, *Space Station Seventh Grade* (Boston: Little, Brown, 1982).

[15]*Bull Durham*, directed by Ron Shelton, 1988, motion picture.

come-down from her dreams of academic life.[16] The great bulk of the novel takes place prior to this job. She has survived difficult personal problems, and as a re-entry student, earned a Harvard Ph.D. in English. By the time she gets her degree, the job market has dried up, and "Nobody wanted to hire a woman over forty." She walks the beach every day, thinking she may be losing her mind, and she drinks too much, but given her determination, intelligence and preparation, she may be an OK teacher, despite her disappointment.

In the murder mystery *Blood Marks*, a young woman applies for an adjunct (part-time) teacher's position at three community colleges in and around Houston.[17] Although many of the faculty characters I found are also part-time teachers, Bill Crider's book is the only fiction that addresses their exploitation by the two-year college system, a common phenomenon at present. The other works add the characteristic "part-time" as just another low-status marker. This central character, divorced and supporting a young daughter, is portrayed sympathetically. Before she can be given the opportunity to race between three campuses for little money and no fringe benefits, she must wait until the semester starts, the full-time teachers all have the courses they need, and the T.B.A. courses fill. Even so, she defends the two-year college and its students when an opinionated and nasty neighbor says, "They used to be *junior* colleges, and that's what they are— not the real thing." We will not be surprised if this speaker, who is so quick to vilify the community colleges, turns out to be the murderer at the end of the mystery.

---

[16]Marilyn French, *The Women's Room* (New York: Simon & Schuster, 1977), 500.

[17]Bill Crider, *Blood Marks* (New York: St. Martin's Press, 1991), 46.

So while the heroine does not actually begin teaching before the book ends, during the climax, on an empty community college campus parking lot on a rainy night, she defends her daughter, saves both their lives by seriously wounding the serial killer, and finds romance with another and much nicer neighbor. Tough and resourceful, this woman can become at least an OK teacher.

Of the thirty faculty members that I located in fiction, several marry or have affairs with a student of theirs who is the central character in the work. As interesting as this may be, we learn little about their teaching or their college in the process. Michael on *Thirtysomething* has an affair with his English teacher;[18] an assistant community college librarian in North Carolina, a gentle and sympathetic man, is married happily to a former student in the novel *Raney*;[19] and Dr. Bernie Ripman of Miami, yet another English teacher, this time in Appalachia, marries the central character at the end of *Oral History*.[20] They then leave for Chicago. His assignment of an oral history of her Hoot Owl Holler family constitutes a large part of the book.

Probably-Not-So-OK Teachers

The creative writing teacher in *Throw Mama from the Train*, a Yale graduate, is not very effective with his class of multi-aged students at Valley College in California.[21] He does, however, refuse to aid a student who wants his mother murdered. The student feels that his professor, since he is "crea-

---

[18]*Thirtysomething*, 1991, television series.

[19]Edgerton, *Raney*.

[20]Smith, *Oral History*.

[21]*Throw Mama From the Train*, 1990, motion picture.

tive," could commit the perfect crime. The teacher is roman-
tically interested in an anthropology professor at the same
school, who seems more stable and effective than he, and she
may be a better teacher. We are shown no evidence either way.
At the end of the movie, the English teacher has overcome
his writer's block and published a book based on the student's
unsuccessful murder plot.

Mary Tyler Moore, in one episode of the *Mary Tyler
Moore Show*, takes a night class in order to improve her
writing.[22] She thinks the teacher is unfair when he lowers her
grade because he expects more from her than from the other
students. During an episode of *Reasonable Doubts*, an alcoholic English professor courts a student of his in a bar.[23] He
feels very sad about his lot, condemned to a community
college. A part-time accounting teacher in *The Hero of New
York* is called a "well-dressed turd" by Charlie, the central
character of the novel, but the name-caller is a student whose
opinion is not always to be trusted.[24]

In *Anagrams*, by Laurie Moore, the central character is
a punning and fantasizing instructor in New York who tells
us, "You might one day wake up and find yourself teaching
at a community college; there will have been nothing to warn
you. You might say things to your students like, There is only
one valid theme in literature: Life will disappoint you."[25]
While we do not meet her students, it is unlikely they benefit
from this teaching.

In a meant-to-be-funny Joyce Carol Oates short story,
"Angst," the names alone of community college teachers are

---

[22]"The Mary Tyler Moore Show," 1990, television series.

[23]"Reasonable Doubts," 1992, television series.

[24]Coughlin, *The Hero of New York.*

[25]Lorrie Moore, *Anagrams* (New York: Alfred Knopf, 1986), 63.

used to let us know how low status they are and how embarrassed the central character is to have them comprise the audience at a Modern Language Association panel discussion of her fiction.[26] To her chagrin, the Ivy League types go to hear her enemy, a trendy literary critic. For instance, *her* audience includes Bobbie Rae Dean of Lamar Tech., Jolene Snyder of Milwaukee C. C. and Rodney Wong of St. Clair Tech., while two males, D. J. Fox of Princeton and E. Cleary of Columbia (note the tasteful initials) head for the enemy's much larger group in the ballroom of a Chicago hotel. Worse yet, her panel is all female except for one person, Erich Larson, who is from a small community college in New Rochelle. He gives a paper that gets her writing totally wrong. It is this "delicate and precious" writer's dreaded nightmare, and we infer that Larson and his colleagues would be no better as teachers.

The English teacher at squalid Highland Park Junior College near Detroit in another Oates work, *Them*, may be just tired or discouraged.[27] He is a shabby graduate student at Wayne State University and has a wife and three children. Some people describe him as kind. When he leaves his family in order to marry a student of his, the central character, he acts as if he is in a dream, hardly aware of his actions. His teaching is no more energized or thoughtful.

A short story called "Stripping" centers around an exotic dancer who applies for a P.E. position at a Texas community college.[28] She does not take the job, but the faculty member

---

[26] Joyce Carol Oates, "Angst," in *The Hungry Ghosts* (Los Angeles: Black Sparrow Press, 1975).

[27] Oates, *Them*.

[28] Jim Sanderson, "Stripping," *Ellipsis* 1, no. 3 (Campbell, CA: Ellipsis Press, 1989).

who interviews her is shallow and mundane, his hair moussed until it "looks like styrofoam." He *can't* be a good teacher, given the level of his comments to her and the tacky moral messages he chooses to run on the electric Coca Cola sign outside the school.

Poor Teachers/Bad Guys

In the detective story *Miami Blues*, a writing teacher at Miami-Dade ignores or insults his students.[29] Susan, the central character, a business major and hooker, brings her psychopathic killer boyfriend to class once, since Mr. Turner never recognizes anyone anyway. Turner is bored and sarcastic, teaching haiku to thirty-five sullen students. Mr. Turner's role was eliminated in the movie made of *Miami Blues* in 1989.[30]

Another detective story, Edward Mackin's *The Nominative Case*, is one of the rare works that is actually set in a two-year college.[31] Unfortunately, Lyndon B. Johnson Community College in New York City is not believable as described. Among other things, it has the beginning remedial students common to inner-city schools; however, the detective who is called in to solve the case had the same faculty in the same rooms advise him during his failed attempt at writing a doctoral dissertation in English. Faculty in New York have told me this is hardly likely.

Even more unfortunately, the faculty are corrupt and cynical. Professor Frye, the English teacher who is the central

---

[29]Willeford, *Miami Blues*.

[30]*Miami Blues*, 1989, motion picture.

[31]Mackin, *The Nominative Case*, 87.

character, gives capricious, inaccurate lectures on Milton to his students, like "automatic writing," he says, since they are so ignorant he feels he can get away with anything. "The slumbering beast only wakes up if the antinomian prejudices of the day are questioned."[32] There is no "community" in a community college, he says. "They should offer their courses on TV and get it over with." Faculty and staff hold the college and its students in contempt. The author may have meant to show how clever and intellectually superior the faculty are, especially compared to their students, but they seem arch and despicable instead. One of them is the murderer, and his victim, another faculty member, is an unlikable wretch whose death evokes little pity.

My last two examples of bad teachers are both white male English teachers, the fictional archetype for community college faculty. They are petty and ignoble. In the first example, the narrator in *Ella Price's Journal* has an affair with her English professor at Bay City Junior College in northern California.[33] He is not totally ineffective as a teacher, since he assigns the journal that forms the whole of the novel, and writing the journal proves to be a liberating act for Ella. She falls in love with Professor Harkin and is sexually aroused by the thought of him. However, her actual encounters with him are so brief and brutal they feel like rape, and it turns out he exploits his re-entry women students on a regular basis. He has sex with a different woman each semester; his male colleagues call them his "worn-out weepers." She learns of this after he has dropped her, and she overhears his seduction of the next victim.

---

[32]Ibid., p. 55.

[33]Bryant, *Ella Price's Journal.*

Professor Harkin believes in Burton Clark's "cooling-out" theory and sees his job as easing out the losers so that they won't revolt against a society that keeps them from a "decent life." The losers are the great majority, in his estimation. He is bitter about his role, but does little to change it or the situation.

The second novel introduces the community college faculty member in the epilogue. In Garrison Keillor's *WLT: A Radio Romance*, we meet a would-be felon, a mass communications professor from a New Hampshire junior college who is writing a biography of the central character, a famous radio and television newscaster who is now retired.[34] Professor Shell (Professor "Empty") has been working on the biography for two years and has been totally ignored by his subject. The professor is under the delusion that he has writing ability and anticipates fame and fortune. In order to increase sales of the book, he plots the murder of his subject. He will make it look like suicide and thus achieve a smash ending to his scandal-mongering work. While wandering the streets of Manhattan, daydreaming of the millions he will make, he is hit by a truck and turned into a brainless vegetable. He is put into a nursing home near his college, and the only evidence of his manuscript remains on a computer disk. His students have thoughts of transcribing it as a memorial, but then school lets out and they all go home.

Summary

1. The typical two-year college faculty character is a white male English instructor.

---

[34]Garrison Keillor, *WLT: A Radio Romance* (New York: Viking, 1991).

2. Compared to faculty at four-year colleges and universities, the two-year college teacher is almost invisible in American fiction.

3. Teaching is incidental, barely mentioned, in many of the works containing characters who are identified as two-year college faculty. Thus, we can only surmise their quality as teachers, based on other facets of their lives.

4. The rare good teachers work hard to provide their students with an education, trying to be rigorous, but fair. Most are also concerned with promoting transfer to a four-year school and with upward mobility in the work world.

5. The same increase in numbers of faculty characters occurs in the 1980s and 1990s as it does with student characters, and the same shift to portrayals in the mass media rather than in literary works occurs as well.

6. The most common tone is mockery, the most common genre comedy.

Chapter 6

Faculty Journals

I want to rise. And push everything up with me as I go.

Michael Wilson's line for Esperanza in *Salt of the Earth*[1]

T he most striking and consistent theme that emerges
from a reading of the faculty journals is the sense of
mission that these women have. Not the official "Mission
Statement of the College" that a few of them discuss, but a
purposeful, self-directed determination to teach well in order
to help their students (and themselves) "rise up." They wish
to set high standards for their students (and themselves), and
then, through time-giving and caring professionalism, help
everyone reach those standards.

---

[1] Michael Wilson, scriptwriter, *Salt of the Earth* (Old Westbury, NY: Feminist
Press, 1978), 82.

The student journals comment often on this quality. The faculty they admire have a mission and are then tough, but fair, in order to accomplish it.

> My experience with the instructors in particular has been very positive. They welcome the enthusiasm and desire to learn that an adult student brings to class. The relationships I have developed with my instructors have been encouraging and supportive. They understand and relate to the struggles that go along with raising a family and managing school, and I really appreciate their encouragement. What is so wonderful is that they see the desire and respond. I would say this has been the case with the majority of my teachers. (OK2)

> I needed three letters of recommendation, and asked my favorite teachers, whose classes I truly enjoyed. In spite of their busy schedules, each took the time and effort to write an eloquent letter. This is another example of the personal involvement of the faculty with their students. I chose each one because I admired their teaching abilities. I learned so much in each of their classes. However, the more valuable lesson learned was their personal style and technique of teaching. I hope I can emulate each of them in developing my own style. The learning experience here is not all academic. It consists of teachers who care, give positive encouragement and help us strive to accomplish our goals. I have been exposed to new ideas and old, and I have learned as much about people as I have about the subject matter. (DA2)

> I think the teachers take on so much. Not only do they work in the classroom, they work at counseling a lot of people in their classes too. I've gotten to know a lot of my teachers and they have helped me sort out a lot of stuff in my life. Where do these women *come* from? (SY1)

Before I discuss the faculty journals further, let us see where these women do come from. Literally, they are from seven states and two other countries (Germany and Mexico), holding nine master's degrees and five doctorates. All but one journal writer described her career path on the way to her full-time teaching position at a two-year college. Two actually started as community college students themselves, and I will discuss their stories in detail later in this chapter. It should be understood that the faculty the students praise or damn are not the same faculty who wrote journals, with two exceptions. Students and faculty are at the same colleges, of course, and the two exceptions are students who praised two of their teachers without knowing that they, too, were writing a journal for this book.

Seven of the fourteen faculty women have held jobs outside of teaching, mostly in other service professions or in management positions. One, the oldest writer, took early retirement the year she wrote the journal and is now working in another profession in another state. She, more than the others, traces the development of the two-year system from junior college to community college, as she experienced it at her school. Her situation, taking early retirement, is a common practice at present. The system offers the opportunity of leaving to those who are paid a living wage, in order to replace them with those who are not—adjunct or part-time faculty.

Although all five colleges are unionized, only four writers mentioned the union, three positively (as protection against capricious management) and one negatively (as a male club mainly interested in protecting its most senior members). Two of the most common words in the journals are "freedom" (to teach) and "overload" (courses, papers, etc.). The faculty are grateful for the former and despairing of the latter. The union is sometimes mentioned in connection with both words.

As I wrote earlier, all fourteen women faculty who agreed to keep a journal for me did so. They wrote an average of nine and one-half typewritten pages each, a little more than the students did. The faculty were more likely to use a word processor instead of writing by hand in the books that I gave them, and that may help account for the greater length, along with the obvious expectation that an experienced teacher would be a more fluent writer than most undergraduates. Their entries, in addition, were usually much less personal than those of the students; mostly, they wrote about their public lives in relation to their colleges and to their students. This suited my purpose well, although I did not ask for it specifically.

Their average age was forty-seven, ranging from forty to fifty-eight, and they have been teaching an average of eighteen years each. I wanted people who were very experienced with the two-year college system, and I certainly got them. Six of the teachers were from the social sciences, four from the humanities, and one each from physical science, nursing, mathematics, and criminal justice. Nine were married, thirteen had children, and ten of the thirteen had two children apiece. Two had four children each, the largest number any faculty writer had.

As is true of the student writers, their racial and ethnic backgrounds were consistent with the percentages within their own colleges and also among two-year colleges in the United States in general. Ten women were white, three African-American, and one a Latina. However, it is rare that a writer's race or ethnicity is apparent from her journal, and it is almost as rare to be able to discern the race, ethnicity or geographical location of the students they write about.

Some of them have published articles or written papers for conferences, but they all see themselves primarily as teachers. Although they do not use the phrase "having a calling," it is clear that some of them mean just that when they speak of "mission." Several began their journals with a brief synopsis of childhood, when they already knew that teaching was their life's goal. These particular writers are not the "accidental careerists" that Sylvia Mann writes about women who somehow wind up in professions, unplanned,[2] although there are a few among the fourteen writers who came upon their "mission" later in life. OK5: "Teaching isn't something I *do*. Teaching is who I am. Oh, I'm wife, mother, friend, etc., but professionally, I am a teacher."

Almost all of them write about further educating themselves, through course work and other means, during their teaching careers. They are a questioning group, consistently examining their techniques, their colleges, and their own efficacy.

In the journals written by students, faculty are both damned and praised, as one might expect, but praise is more than twice as frequent. Here are some typical complaints: SY1: "Some teachers make you wonder why they even bother to be here." SY4: "Not all teachers are dedicated and/or committed on the same level." SY3: "I never realized before that some professors might be threatened by me."

Here is some typical praise: OK9: "Ordinarily, I would never think of missing a class, but with such outstanding instructors, the need to attend is even greater, and very exciting." DA7: "The instructor demands respect from her stu-

---

[2] Sylvia Mann, "Complementarity, Dissonance and Awakening: Major Themes in the Career Lives of Women in Traditional Occupations" (Ed.D. diss., Northern Illinois University, 1991).

dents, and is very helpful to those who are in need of help."
SY3: "The reputation of our instructors is getting out. They're
dedicated people who want the students to learn what they're
teaching." HW8: "It is nice to hear from others that you are
not a stupid person, and that you can move ahead and have a
good career with good opportunities." DA2: "The instructors
here develop personal relationships with their students that
make for a relaxed, comfortable atmosphere."

> I looked around and saw that I had teachers from Loyola,
> Northwestern and various other status schools. So I know
> that I am much smarter because I am getting the same
> instructors at a fraction of the cost. (OK1)

> I got scared and wanted to withdraw. And then the pro-
> fessor said the magic words, "I'll give you any help you
> need." I was very fortunate. He was just what I needed—
> he not only helped me, but lit a fire under me with his
> enthusiasm for American history that was contagious.
> (OK3)

> I often wonder why some of the women teaching here
> have settled for PCC, but if I look at them and how they
> structure their classes and whatnot, they fit in between
> true Academia and real life experiences. They seem to
> have been here where I am, they understand, whereas
> many "Academia" professors have lost the human ele-
> ment. Here, the professors take into account who is
> writing, what they are saying, and then the logic. It's more
> human. (SY3)

Two Who Played Both Roles

Two of the fourteen writers were once students in community colleges at the very start of their paths to graduate
degrees. They have not forgotten that beginning. In fact, it

forms an important part of their teaching lives at present. I would like to discuss those two career routes in some detail, since the double view these women have is particularly valuable in seeing the image of the two-year college system from the vantage point of its inhabitants.

DA6 first encountered the urban community college in a freezing cold, poorly-lit basement of a local church. As an immigrant from Mexico with three small children, "I knew that learning the language of this country was absolutely necessary." So she started taking evening classes in English as a Second Language at an off-campus site run by a community college. Despite extremely uncomfortable conditions and no books that the students could take home, "The teacher was very patient and dedicated, and I found myself not wanting to miss any of his classes."

A few years later, she was a part-time teacher for the same system, confident that she was the right person for the job.

> I knew what worked and what did not work because I had been there. I had the academic credentials, and, living in the same neighborhood, I was familiar with the cultural and socio-economic problems of my students.
>
> I had a lot of dreams. I began implementing new techniques while teaching. My students kept attending. We were learning from one another, and having fun. I felt great. There was a bond between us that still remains. I have never been able to forget my students. (DA6)

Five years later, she was a full-time faculty member in counseling, with a master's degree. Recruiting for the college in her old neighborhood, she visited some off-campus sites, and

> I was forced to face the cruel reality of the "services" provided to our ESL and GED students. I remember

vividly a "class" that was taking place in a garage, a dirty
old place on the backyard of a house. The dirt floor was
partially covered by a raggedy, filthy "rug," and fumes
emanating from a kerosene heater were nauseating.
Adults were sitting on elementary school-size desks, *two*
to every desk. It was an incredible sight!

I felt pain, anger, frustration and humiliation all at once.
I felt like a hypocrite, standing there telling them that our
college really cared about education. I had a headache
and a heartache. That experience has been one of the most
embarrassing experiences of my life. (DA6)

Her reaction was to take on the administrators of the
system and force them to close down the site. But she contin-
ues to worry about the students who were involved at that
location and persists in her fight against the bureaucracy. "We
must never forget," she writes.

The last entry in her journal is moving to me, despite
frequent readings. In part, this is because she describes a
community college graduation, a ritual that touches me every
year, no matter how bland or ill-equipped the speakers. It is
an event that pointedly reveals the injustice of the "loser"
image bestowed upon the two-year college student by our
fiction and by our culture. In an earlier article I wrote, I
described the audience at a typical graduation ceremony.

Our gym is packed with grandmas in Slavic babushkas
and Arab gowns, parents in suits and in working clothes,
and a lot of kids, including the grown children of our
graduates. Black women wearing outfits out of MGM
musicals arrive late, carrying long-stemmed roses for
their nieces and daughters. It's wonderful theater, and
these people have not come to see losers. They have come
to applaud winners, often the first family member to
attend college, on her or his way up.[3]

DA6 focuses on her own feelings as a former graduate herself, now attending the ceremony as a new full-time faculty member.

> Sheer joy. Marching with the whole faculty for the first time. Greeting the students from the previous semesters. Hugging them. The gym is filled to capacity, relatives dressed in their finest. "Aida" fills the air as the students enter, proud and tall, every one of them. My heart beats a little faster. My mind races back fifteen years. I see myself standing in line, waiting nervously for my name to be called. And then, I feel the pride again. The pride of holding, with trembling hands, my first college degree. (DA6)

MV3 also travelled a long way, although via a different route. Like DA6, she married young, had children, and did not originally plan on getting a college degree. She enrolled at her local community college in order to compete with all the "career women" she imagined her husband would meet as he moved up the educational and professional ladder. One course in sociology with an inspiring professor opened the window onto what she wanted to do. Now, twenty years later, she has a Ph.D. in the discipline and is still in touch with her model and mentor. She is also still married to the same man. "I will be married 27 years this June. Somehow we beat the odds of having a successful marriage."

The two-year college available to her when she started in higher education has the initials O.C.C., which lends itself to a derisive nickname that compares to the disparaging names given to the five schools I used for this book: "Old Calamity College." Even with the school's low reputation,

---

[3] Nancy LaPaglia, "The Missing Majority: The Community College in American Fiction." In *Model Voices* (New York: McGraw Hill, 1989), 446.

she was afraid of her ability to succeed in any school and at first took one course at a time that she was sure she could pass. (This from a woman who impressed me with her strength and assurance. Her visual image reinforces that impression, as she is tall, wears cowboy boots, and drives a pick-up truck.) For example, she had lived in Germany for several years while her husband was in the military, so she took beginning German. When an advanced German course was canceled later on, she substituted sociology, and, she writes, "The rest is history."

She recounts her educational background in great detail, "because it has had such a profound influence on my own attitude toward community colleges," even though she could have afforded nothing else. The camaraderie and encouragement of other students contributed to her success, and the interest, accessibility, and support of the instructors impressed her. Despite further education and teaching experience at an expensive private school and a major state university, she does not consider two-year colleges "second-rate." "The idea that 'anybody can go there' might have something to do with the negative attitude, but it seems to me that the nature of 'community' is one of non-exclusiveness."

She tells the story of her educational start during an introductory lecture to each new class, as a way of counteracting the derogatory image she and the students are aware of. She tells them they are smart enough to reject the label, and smarter still to get a good education at much less cost.

> It never fails but that a number of students come up at the end of class and thank me for the speech. I have even had students tell me two semesters later how much that speech meant to them and how much it inspired them. (MV3)

She feels that there are fewer students who are academically ill-prepared for college at the four-year schools, but just as many who are socially unprepared to assume the responsibilities of a college student. "Really bright, capable students, every instructor's dream" exist in both systems.

She passed up a chance to teach at a well-known liberal arts college when she got her doctorate ("I thought my dissertation advisor was going to strangle me"), partly because an offered community college position was "a bird in hand," but also because she knew where she would have the greatest impact. She and a colleague at another two-year school agree that if they really believe in the mission of sociology (as they see it, to bring a sense of class consciousness to "the masses"), then a community college is the best place to teach.

> Community college students need good, dedicated teachers, not good researchers or famous professors. We concluded that community college students would have to get by in this world with what they know, not who they know, and that was enough justification for what we were doing. It sure sounds pretty good, but I am still embarrassed sometimes to tell people I teach at a community college. And I hate to admit that I am embarrassed. Some old habits of thought die hard. I think it is just the way people respond sometimes—usually they just say, 'Oh,' when I tell them where I teach. (MV3)

Therefore, her greatest complaint is that she is not given a sense of respect and dignity by her own college administration. This is a common complaint of the faculty journal writers. Many of them *chose* to teach at two-year schools, they have an incredible teaching load and paper-grading load, budget cuts are causing additional pressures, and society in general considers them beneath notice. At the very least, they should be treated as professionals by their own administrators, and they are not.

She, as every other journal writer, searches for ways to help the poorly-prepared student "rise up." She discusses constant nurturing, bonding, and the necessity of teaching college survival skills to the large number who lack them. "I have always felt that at the community college you sometimes have to 'reach down,' but not 'teach down'."

Her journal ends, as did DA6's, on a personal note. In her case, despite her sincere belief that she is performing a valuable service to her community, she needs to know that she has a place among the "big boys" of higher education, though they will not acknowledge it. She uses two metaphors to express her thoughts.

> You know, it's a funny thing. There might exist a strange kind of feedback loop out there. The people at the big universities get to do all the research, get the grants, make the "breakthroughs" in the social sciences, but how it gets taught to the vast majority of people—how it gets interpreted to the masses, is often in the hands of the teaching professionals. We act as the "filters for knowledge," and it is our version of knowledge that reaches a great many people. Who then are the real educators, the real opinion makers? (MV3)

Both of these women, from colleges far apart geographically and in other ways, resent the marginal status assigned to them and to their students by the culture. Both feel that the administrators of their schools acquiesce in that demeaning opinion, and both see themselves as embarked on a life-long mission: a mission to nurture, to set decent standards, to question themselves and others, to educate themselves and their students. Like Esperanza ("Hope") in *Salt of the Earth*, they want to rise, and push everything up with them as they go.

A Sense of Mission

For the faculty journal writers, to succeed or to win, to overcome one's assigned marginal status, means to cooperate, to join hands with others, with everyone, so that all will win. The alternative, to succeed at the *expense* of others, to gain altitude by stepping on other people, does not fit their mission.

They are not martyrs, neglecting their own needs so that others may succeed, but are interested in satisfying their own needs *along* with others. Jill Ker Conway, who researches women's autobiographies, says that quite different themes emerge from them than from men's autobiographies.[4] Men are interested in conquest, testing their manhood against a society from which they feel alienated. Women are more likely to succeed in reform movements, where a nurturing mission replaces the male quest. Conway adds that women usually give some of the credit for their success to luck and thank others for their part; men often give themselves *too much* credit, disregarding chance and other people. The women journal writers in this study fit Conway's model for women autobiographers in both respects. They are on a nurturing mission, and they share the credit for any success.

They do not seek pity for their status or their situation. A current magazine article states that "Women customarily see themselves as victims of men, and even, one might argue, enjoy doing so, to the degree that the victim's degraded status

---

[4] Jill Ker Conway, in a lecture at the Oriental Institute, University of Chicago, January 1992.

can be confused with the blamelessness necessary to moral
superiority."[5] I agree that this attitude can be dangerously
popular today among the marginalized of all kinds, dangerous
even if understandable in the light of history. But I never heard
that tone in these journals. Anger, yes, confrontation, sometimes, but not whining or holier-than-thou victimology or
demonology. ("It's all the fault of the demons; I'm just a
victim.") The writers never seem to seek pity; they just lay it
out as they see it—the situation they and their students are
in—with the passion appropriate to those on a mission.

Twelve of the fourteen write about questioning their own
methodologies or their abilities or their philosophies of education. They educate themselves; they are looking for better
ways to teach, to grade, to work with colleagues. They wish
to set a fire under themselves and everyone else, and they
understand that this is difficult to do. They want a revolution
in the politics of education. HW6: "How about some forward-
thinking innovative educators to devise constructive solutions to our problems? Now I'm really dreaming." But she is
excited by the prospect, and she actively organizes other
faculty in order to make the dream come true.

The idea of working cooperatively with others in order
to accomplish their goals is a common theme, and a commonly expressed pleasure as well.

> I feel very close to other faculty. They are supportive and
> non-competitive. Those who are deeply invested in the
> institution have a level of responsibility that is virtually
> unmanageable. I see coordination, care, attention, and
> belief in the role among faculty in a group I am working

---

[5] Elizabeth Kaye, "What I Think of Other Women," *Esquire*, August 1992,
100.

with. We're all on our best behavior, yet there is real disagreement and debate. Just no hostility. (OK4)

The other faculty are a good support group. Civilized. That's lucky, since we have no privacy, and the entire department shares one telephone and one large office. (SY9)

Some of those who work cooperatively also have other missions in addition that are more specific and personal.

I am in a non-traditional discipline for a woman, and I have a REAL MISSION in this area: Fighting Dirty Harry and Lethal Weapon and all of the crap on TV. I hope to make some inroads in some brains as far as fairness, equity, equality and justice are concerned.

I have never felt that community college students are not "real" students, but I am fighting sexism, careerism, some laziness and some pigheaded stupidity. My idol is Richard Quinney, not Darryl Gates. Many have a problem understanding how radical criminology (not to mention the criminology of peacemaking) has any relevance to what-they-assume-will-be-dangerous lives on the line, guns drawn against that horde of marauding blacks determined to sell their children drugs.

I love empowering people who have felt excluded. I believe, with Mark Lane, that the way the media controls how understanding of social change is framed is terrifying. Susan Faludi has said it all. (MV4)

Nurturing and Generative Actions

Faculty write about nurturing their students as professionals rather than as "moms." They try to provoke in their students the effort and the thought that will beget more "engaged learners." They offer energy, focus, emotion, and intelligence. "No-nonsense" is a frequent description they choose for themselves. OK5 learns everyone's name quickly; "No one plays non-committal sponge in my class." DA1, working in a hospital setting, says, "Through intimate contact with students and patients, a relationship develops that's based on sharing life's dramas. Sounds insipid, but true."

Despite an incredible overload of 250 students per semester, SY9 has a personal conference with each student at the end of the course in order to show them their accomplishments. "It's tough work, but a natural high, to step back and gain some perspective. In theory, it's for them, but in fact, I think it's equally *gratifying* for me!" HW2 tries to show students she doesn't always live up to her *own* expectations, as a way of encouraging them to try even when they are afraid of failing.

DA5 thinks that math anxiety "transcends all cultural, socio-economic and ethnic boundaries." So she invented ROEYAKs. Students were told there would be no more quizzes, only a frequent ROEYAK (Review of Everything You Already Know). Scores rose. In another entry, she tells of a thirty-five-year-old student who came in with a note from her daughter, a high school student who helped the mother with her homework. The note accused the teacher of being mean for assigning so much work and causing her mother to cry every night. The "accused" took the note seriously, met with both women, worked with the mother, encouraged the daughter to think about a career as a math teacher, and was happy that the mother finished the course with a high grade. This nurturer does not take credit for what happened; it's just part of the job. "I continue to marvel at the splendor of watching yet another mathematical worm turn into a butterfly." She chose this incident as an entry because it was an interesting anecdote; the note came from a child instead of a parent.

HW6 may take a tougher line. "You pay me," she tells her students. "Get your money's worth. I'll make as many steps as you make. I won't drag you, but I'll match you." She talks tough, but her journal and her later interview are filled with nurturing metaphors such as "planting seeds," "nurturing the soil," "turning students around," and "going the extra mile when the window is open." She tries to help poor test takers, or a robbery victim, a shooting witness, the friend of an AIDS patient, and students who have lost their mothers. She celebrates those who make it. She is angry at a society that does not recognize their worth and fights the board of trustees on the students' behalf. She is tough and demanding of everyone, including herself.

Marginality

Every faculty journal discusses the marginality of their students, both as it is experienced by the students and as it is perceived by the larger culture. In addition, about half of them write about their own assigned marginality as two-year college teachers. Inside the system they are all business; outside they are aware of their low status.

Three women chose to write a list of the kinds of students they had in one class at the time of the journal (or as it could be in any semester), in order to illustrate clearly the diversity, the problems, and the fascination of their students and their human dramas. I will reproduce these lists, but first, two comments: (1) Most two-year college teachers will accept these lists as truthful and will not see them as bizarre; and (2) any two-year college, either mostly white or mostly minority, can produce such lists. Some schools have fewer students who are at the extreme financial margin, but one of the following lists is from the wealthiest school. There are problems, and there are problems.

> Among the students in one speech class are an extremely talented male senior citizen, a young South American undergoing chemotherapy for breast cancer, a Vietnamese young woman who'd spent a year hiding in the jungle subsisting on rice, an 18-year-old male just out of a psychiatric ward after trying to commit suicide, several who'd flunked out of 4-year schools and were trying to pick up their grades, and three Americans who'd joined the class as a "team," thinking it would be easy. (From suburban Illinois)

> Among my current students is one whose husband kidnapped their child overseas and left her with only the clothes on her back, one who gave up custody of her three young children so she could go to school, one who works three minimum wage jobs to keep in school, and a single mother on welfare rooked by a proprietary school, and now with no credits to show for it owes $4,000 for one quarter, of which she attended three weeks. The "official" budgetary concerns of the school pale in comparison. (From Oregon)

> I'm working with a campus service club trying to clothe the needy children of our students. Hope we have enough clothes by Christmas. They are struggling with overwhelming family difficulties, while I'm trying to teach them to write complete sentences and complete their assignments on time.

> The community college has become a dumping ground for social services, since it is one of the few agencies left providing a variety of services. This semester a colleague and I have counseled students with psychiatric problems,

head injuries, hallucinations, aggression towards children, drug and alcohol abuse (in recovery and not in
recovery), learning disabilities, and victims of rape and
child abuse. It is overwhelming. [Note: She and her
colleague are not counselors.] (From upstate New York)

A fourth teacher, at an urban campus, does not make one
single list, but she speaks of students who have encountered
rape, armed robbery, death, AIDS, frequent car accidents, and
of one who was a witness to a killing and is struggling with
the shock. A middle-class African-American herself, this
faculty member believed the amount of trauma in the lives of
these students only after witnessing it. She continued the
theme in a later meeting that we had.

[In an interview] Now, when I talk to trustees, when I talk
to people with money or authority who can help, I am a
translator. They think these people are lazy, they think
they're shiftless, they think they don't *want* any better.
They don't understand that when your mother who is on
welfare dies, you're in a different place than I am if *my*
mama dies. 'Cause my mama probably left *me* something. Your mama left you *nothing*. Maybe three, four,
five kids to care for, or whatever. And the trustees say,
they just drop out for no reason. And they *believe* this,
these people. So I see myself as a translator in the middle
of this *chaos*. (From Chicago)

The faculty are aware of the marginal status of their
colleges among the general public. One thinks that the worst
thing for the students is the perception held by many that the
community college is second-rate, and that the popular view
may be an impediment to student success, or, even worse, may
keep some from attending who could greatly benefit. She
feels things are changing too slowly. Another reports an
overheard conversation in a restaurant between father and

son. "'I can get into Colgate, no sweat. Don't worry, Dad, I won't go to MVCC.' We're seen as such a dumping ground, and yet we do so much good."

A teacher in Oregon writes that higher tuition at the state universities has increased the number of reverse transfers and better-prepared high school graduates attending two-year schools. She feels that this may improve their popular image. Many faculty give a portrayal of a stigmatized student body and faculty, together confronting a society oriented to the four-year system in order to be seen as "worthy." One dissenting writer, however, feels that, "The students don't trust us, because they've been lied to and rejected. They may not even be aware of their political position, or see us as allies against the system."

Several faculty, like the politicized students in Chapter 4, organize. They are active in or sponsor women's groups; some arranged a controversial teach-in against the Gulf War in an extremely conservative part of the country; they fight administrators insensitive to racism; and they work for abortion rights and other feminist causes. Several state specifically that they think the two-year college is belittled at least partly because the students are primarily female. Most of them see diversity as a positive characteristic and try to teach others what that means to a college, or could mean. There is little evidence that these teachers have blindly internalized the stigma society tries to place upon them, and many indications that they are active resisters against the demeaning image.

While they are likely to see their mission as spiritual or ethical or intellectual, they also recognize the economic marginality of many students. As Annie Dillard writes in one of her essays when she quotes a West African proverb, "The beginning of wisdom is to get you a roof."[6]

In my field, the community college enables students to begin a career with a salary adequate to raise a family and have a fairly decent life. The community college is the real world. It assists real people in their lives, hopefully enriching those lives in some fashion.

I keep thinking about that academic snob from the University of Chicago that has made his life's work out of misunderstanding the community college—I forget his name. Then I think of the long lines of students waiting to register for their courses—immigrants, old people . . . all looking so hopeful . . . a start . . . accessible, financially feasible, leading one to whatever they want, be it English 101 or a degree in nursing. (DA1)

Poorly-Prepared Students and Other Problems

No journal writer denies the existence of real problems in the two-year college system. Theirs is not "the undisciplined optimism forever bobbing to the surface," commonly encountered in education, according to one adult education researcher.[7] The problem that appears the most frequently is the lack of preparation for college-level work that many students bring to the two-year college. Eight of the faculty writers address this problem at length in terms of academic preparation; four writers discuss the lack of social or emotional preparation (including the use of the community college as a dumping ground for the previously institutionalized); and three examine other serious problems that leave students poorly prepared for college work.

---

[6] Annie Dillard, *The Writing Life* (New York: Harper & Row, 1989), 27.

[7] C. H. Grattan, *In Quest for Knowledge* (New York: Association Press, 1955), 92.

[Describing a student] She is so lively, so ready to learn, so primed for the contagion of knowledge, I wonder how anyone can resist trucking out their best stuff. But most are so ill-prepared they're a long missionary project. Who let them slip by without making the kinds of demands made by people who love one another and expect excellence? (OK4)

Our students are often unprepared. They fail courses for which they are not ready, which serves to reinforce their poor self-image and does nothing to help them achieve their goals. It is hard for them to balance a full load and family obligations, also. (HW1)

I'd love to spend the time expanding their minds, enlightening their spirits, but they need some basics. So you teach the basics, but it's important to teach sometimes to where you want them to be, by intertwining music and books that give hints of what else is available to them once they become *engaged learners*. Teaching without feeding students' spirits, I cannot do. I think oppressed minorities and recent immigrants are more interesting to teach than the privileged of this country. (HW6)

One writer thinks that the student body became more poorly prepared for college in the 1970s. When she wrote the following, she was not describing minority groups.

The ill-prepared arrived as "clients" rather than students. They were paid to attend college by reason of poverty, educational disadvantage, physical handicaps, and, in some cases, emotional and mental dysfunction. New strategies were needed to teach those without basic skills and whose knowledge was essentially informed by TV.

"Feelings" represent authenticity—things are true or not true "because that's the way I feel about it." The walking wounded are denied both the skills that would make them competent, and the quality of mind that experiences life as a wonderful, challenging and interesting journey. (MV11)

The teachers tackle this problem in ways that were described earlier in this chapter. In the face of its magnitude, most of them complain of overload. And overload plus maintaining high standards brings more difficulties. SY9: "I graded papers constantly during the Thanksgiving holiday. I honestly *cannot* teach writing unless they write, I react, they revise—over and over."

> Our mission is misunderstood by the community. We offer quality education to students home from the four-year colleges all the time. I am careful to make my chemistry courses rigorous when they will be accepted by the major universities when the students transfer. In general education, I reach down more, towards an educated citizenry. (HW1)

Complaints about administrators appeared earlier in this chapter, and there are many more. Perhaps grousing about management is traditional in all occupations. I have never been in a faculty group at any level of higher education that did not complain about the administration and about the poor preparation of their students. I am not discounting these grievances, but for all their criticism, the writers mention taking pleasure in their academic freedom as often as they mention the burden of over-loaded schedules. This freedom is one of the reasons they persist despite the stigma accorded their profession. They express their own joy of learning, and more are optimistic than not.

Is this a dignified thing to do with your life, teaching in a two-year college? Most would answer yes. They may differ from each other in their approaches to education and in the image they hold of the two-year college, but like good literature, good teachers are not formulaic—they are individuals with individual stories.

The feeling that I got after reading and re-reading these stories is that I love these people. I am often touched or moved by the *student* writers; I admire them and I want to know the next event in the plot of their lives. But these fourteen teachers make me proud to be on a community college faculty. After reading their journals, it is difficult to imagine why they are so demeaned.

I cannot do better than to end this chapter with the last journal entries of three writers from three different parts of our country. The first is from the East, the second from the West Coast, and the third from the Mid-West.

> I was raised to see "college professor" as the ultimate in career and personal achievement. I have a real sense of personal accomplishment. I am no more than a closet scholar, but a master teacher, in a community college with a "real" college atmosphere, in that teaching is respected. There is freedom from many rules, and I am not teaching career success as much as thinkers-who-can-earn-a-living-for-themselves.

> Overall, I am very grateful for this academic life. Few people are being hired now with only M.A.'s. We make an enormous mistake if we let the "college" part suffer in some trendy following of what "community" is. Hey, here we're struggling with newly released mental patients and ex-cons, since our county is a state-wide dumping ground for these troubled folks. Offer every kind of possible service, yes, but when you get into my class, expect to read books and write papers. (MV4)

> Recently I attended my thirtieth high school reunion. I felt proud and fortunate to be able to say that I was a community college teacher, and felt that "doing this"

with my life was as important and rewarding as anything anyone else was doing—more so, in most cases. And this was among a group of privileged and successful women. (SY5)

"It was the best of times, it was the worst of times." I love the job, the fresh starts three times a year. The community college adds a dimension unique to itself: The diversity of the population, not only in terms of who they are, but also in what talents and abilities each has, and what the spectrum is of objectives, motives and baggage from their past experiences. The open-door policy makes good on Emma Lazarus' words.

There is more best than worst. My relationship with the community college is filling and fulfilling. Take away all the trimmings, and what it boils down to is that the best is a classroom of students, enough materials to teach them, and the opportunity for me to say, "My name is [____]. Welcome to [XYZ] 101. It's going to be one of the best classes you'll ever have in college—I hope, and I'm your teacher. Now, let's get into it!" (OK5)

Summary

1. Faculty write consistently about their sense of mission. They wish to set high standards for their students and themselves and then help everyone reach those standards. They take pride in being teachers and fight for their students and themselves.

2. They believe that people succeed or win by cooperating with others, not by conquest. The writers do not see themselves as helpless, pitiful victims, and they do not treat their students as such.

3. They educate themselves throughout their careers, striving to be better at what they do. They nurture their students in a professional manner, in order to help them better themselves.

4. The student writers are critical of some faculty, but they praise far more often, most commonly for caring, for being demanding, and for exciting them with the joy of learning.

5. Faculty are keenly aware of the marginality of their students, both actual and perceived. They recount the human drama of the students' often traumatic lives. The most commonly perceived student problem is poor preparation for college-level work.

6. Comparable images, descriptions, and stories occur in each geographic area, to each racial or ethnic group. It is rarely possible to discern the race or ethnicity of the writers or of the students they write about.

Chapter 7

Writing The Journals

Both fiction and autobiography attempt to impose order on
the only life the writer really knows, his own. Once I heard
someone ask John Cheever why he wrote. He replied
without hesitation, "To try to make sense of my life." That is
the best answer I can conceive of.

Wallace Stegner, *Where the Bluebird Sings to the Lemonade
Springs: Living and Writing in the West*[1]

At first, I anticipated that I would have a lot of trouble
persuading enough people to write journals for me. It
took a lot of nerve on my part, I thought, to approach a total
stranger and ask her to add yet another task to her crowded
days. The lives of the women I wanted as writers, both
students and faculty, were already filled with obligations
imposed on them by others, plus responsibilities that they had

---

[1] Wallace Stegner, *Where the Bluebird Sings to the Lemonade Springs: Living
and Writing in the West* (New York: Random House, 1992), 219.

taken on by choice. Why would they agree to write in a blank book for three weeks and then send it off to someone they did not know in Chicago?

I was surprised to find that getting nearly forty writers was reasonably manageable. Some of the women seemed almost eager to write, they needed little convincing, and they thanked me for allowing them the privilege! I started receiving little notes, sometimes thank-you notes, attached to their books or manuscripts. Why did they write? What could they expect to gain from putting in the time? Why was the return rate so exceptionally high?

All fourteen of the faculty returned their journals, as did twenty-three out of the thirty-three students who had agreed to write. The combined total return rate was 80 percent. Only two women already kept journals at the time that I asked them for the more specifically focused writing I wanted for the book. One of them, a student, was a long-time keeper of a diary, and the other, an English teacher, sometimes used journal writing as a technique in her classes. On those occasions, she would keep a personal journal at the same time as her students. Another faculty member was a former journal keeper, recently become familiar with a word processor.

> Having tried to keep personal journals over the years (and sometimes succeeding), I'm approaching this task with some reluctance. I'm hoping it will be considerably easier with the computer than it ever was with handwriting! (MV4)

Almost every woman wrote at least something about the actual experience of keeping the journal, apart from any specific content pertaining to her life within the two-year college system. A content analysis of these entries generated four different areas that suggest possible answers to the question of why they wrote. The areas are: trying to make sense of their lives, consciously or unconsciously; wanting to be helpful and cooperative for "feminine" reasons; having something they want to say that they think is worth saying; and feeling that the specific "asker" of the favor warranted a positive response.

To Make Sense of One's Life

Cheever and Stegner are among many writers, men and women, who agree that the purpose of writing either fiction or autobiography is to make sense of one's own life. Many of the journal writers thought that the experience of keeping the book did just that.

> Writing about all this has helped me a lot. It has made me realize I'm not much different than anyone else, and it has also been kind of therapeutic for me. As I said before, I wish I had written more, but I wrote what I felt and it's as honest as it can get. (MV5)

> I think I will state my selfish reasons for being part of this evaluation of women in college. My primary reason is to evaluate myself. It seems that thoughts often go round and round in one's head, but once they are put on paper it is easier to see patterns, direction, etc. I have rarely taken the time to write down such thoughts except in letters to family or friends. (SY7)

> I know that this journal made me realize how much I have accomplished and learned in two and a half years. Thank you for giving me the opportunity to relive a lot of the experiences that I have had just to be in school. It makes it much more worth while to keep going. Right now that I look back at my last three semesters, I could see that I learned to struggle and survive my crises. I learned that

I had to do what I had to do, and do it and keep going. (DA9)

I'm in the middle of a life crisis, I think, on a certain professional level. When you asked for the journal, it was like, oh, OK, now I can write it down. I know the value of putting down my thoughts whenever I am *made* to, so it was a good assignment for me, at a good time for me. It clarifies for me. Because I think and move fast, I'm not always on top of where I am. Having to write it gives it some structure. I probably should thank you for giving me the opportunity, for *making* me do it. (HW6)

Sometimes writing the journal gave the author the opportunity to understand something quite specific about her relationship to the two-year college system. MV4: "I hope to spend some time in this journal trying to figure out what difference dorms have made to this campus." The same writer at the end of her book: "This journal has given me the chance to become a little clearer on my own understanding of what a community college is trying to do." HW10: "In reading this over, I realized I had jumped from thinking about taking a business writing class to actually starting a creative writing class." OK1: [Last entry.] "I am giving a presentation tomorrow at the New Student Orientation. I now know what to tell them."

Sometimes what the writer wants to understand is very personal. Journal writing then becomes a method of conversing with one's own inner voice.

This is a very sad day and I am hoping that writing down my thoughts may alleviate some distress. What I am hoping to capsulize here are my responses to complex and deep problems, in hopes of finding some direction or relief within. (SY7)

Such entries are analogous to Northrup Frye's category of "confessional narrative" in some ways,[2] though I never got a sense of a *literal* confession, that I was somehow being allowed to hear of an otherwise unknown personal or family secret. The writers seem to be speaking to themselves at such times. As Gloria Steinem writes in a recent book, "We teach what we need to learn and write what we need to know."[3] The journal writers needed to know about some important aspects of themselves.

To Be Helpful and Cooperative

Some journal writers say they did it because, like many women, they wish to help. OK8: "I appreciate having had the opportunity to participate in this project. I hope what I have written will be of use to you." SY7: "I hope these notes will be of some value to you. It would be most enjoyable to see any results from your findings that you may wish to share." MV5: "Thank you for giving me an opportunity to help you. It made me feel a little important!" OK1: "So I hope this is what you wanted and that it will help you. Good Luck and all my best wishes. Thank you."

Some students saw me as a fellow student or researcher who seemed in need, and they did me a favor by writing. The faculty saw me as a colleague researching a book, and they did the same. These are responsible women, and once they agreed to help, they felt contrite if they did not fulfill their "obligation," or send the book back "soon enough," or write "long enough," or cover the "correct" topics, even though

---

[2] Northrop Frye, *Anatomy of Criticism: Four Essays* (Princeton: Princeton University Press, 1957).

[3] Gloria Steinem, *Revolution from Within* (1992), 6.

what I asked for was open-ended in content and length. Women feel guilty so easily!

I tried hard not to play on this common "female" personality trait. Before my final analysis of the journals, I wrote a letter to everyone, thanking the writers again and trying to let the ten non-writers off the hook. They did not need another millstone of undone chores or another blow to their self-esteem.

I was very grateful for what the writers were doing for me, but I got many apologies from them just the same, especially from the students. OK2: "I hope this is enough. If there is anything else, please feel free to call." SY1: "I hope this helps you a lot (or a little). I wanted to write more, but found myself too busy. Once again, thank you."

> I'm sorry I didn't write more. I was out of commission for three weeks with a ruptured disc in my back and I got behind. If I can do anything else, please contact me at the following phone #. Good luck & best wishes . . . I hope both our dreams are fulfilled. (MV2)

SY8: "Nancy, sorry for the long delay. I'll spare you all of my excuses except that my life has been in constant turmoil the past few months!" HW8: "I'm sorry this is so late! Hope you can still use it."

> Dear Nancy, I am sorry I haven't gotten this done before now. I hope it is not too late for your study. I was laid off work and haven't been focused on this study. I do have another job now and am trying to get caught up. (SYX)

> Wow! A whole week went by, and I don't think I even blinked. I feel bad that I haven't kept up this journal. I made a couple of entries in my personal one, but that doesn't even things out. My apologies. I'll continue to try. (SY3)

[Later entry] I'm not satisfied that I fulfilled my end of the bargain in this writing. I do hope that there is some contribution here. Thank you for asking me to do this. I've enjoyed undertaking it. Best of luck with your endeavor and in all things. (SY3)

There were a few faculty apologies, as well. MV1: "I doubt if I've written enough for three weeks worth, but I'd better get this in the mail to you. Good luck with your dissertation!" DA6: "Just a few entries. Please, let me know if any of my scribbling was useful at all. Thanks."

End of journal effort. In looking back over the entries, they seem mundane, transitory and very trite. Getting a sense of what it means to teach at the c.c. level is very complex, and I'm not sure that I've captured any of it here. But it has been an interesting experience. (SY9)

Overall, however, my first category, writing to understand oneself, and the category that follows, writing to speak out and become part of a larger movement, seem more important than these so-called "feminine" reasons for all of the writers. Deborah Tannen, in a study of linguistics, wrote that men and women speak differently, reflecting their different priorities in life—gaining respect and independence *vs* feeling connected to other people and being liked.[4] The journals suggest strongly that the women who wrote them have both goals—gaining respect *and* feeling connected, and that they imagine the community college as a place where both can happen.

---

[4] Deborah Tannen, *You Just Don't Understand: Women and Men in Conversation* (New York: Morrow, 1990), 24-5.

To Speak Out, and Contribute to a Valued Project

Writing the journals seemed to be a liberating experience for many, not only because they understood themselves and their situation better when they finished, but also because it gave them an opportunity to express views they wanted disseminated to a wider audience. The following writer, for example, reversed her judgement of the two-year college after she enrolled, and she wanted to share that experience.

> I have since changed my negative attitude about this community college. I have instead been quite impressed with what it has to offer. I hope to demonstrate this during my next three weeks of journaling. (OK8)

Many of the faculty writers, with greater emotional charge than the student quoted above, are furious at the constant ridicule the two-year college receives in the media and elsewhere. When I met with each one before they agreed to the project, they expressed pleasure that someone was finally going to look at them from the "inside," and they hoped that the study would be widely read. A typical last note from a faculty writer is the following: SY5: "Good luck with your project—hope to see it in print soon." Or from a student writer: SY1: "Thanks for letting me participate in this. I would like to see the final outcome." This last was written on a piece of stationery with a motto printed at the top: "Sisterhood, like female friendship, has at its core the affirmation of freedom. [Mary Daly]"

Both students and faculty seem to see themselves as parts of *communities* of women. Participating in the study accentuated their feeling of being part of a larger group, contributing to a valuable product, a research project about the two-year colleges. The groups they belong to are usually excluded, and their views are not considered central to society. I offered them the luxury of talking about themselves, of having someone take their opinions seriously. The project made their ideas and convictions legitimate. This book may have been seen as a validation of their worth in some way.

The writers were not asked to be positive about their experiences with the two-year college, and, in my letters to them and when we spoke, I tried to use neutral language. Some were *not* positive. HW10: "I wasn't eager to receive my journal because my first reaction when I heard about the study was that I probably didn't have a lot of good things to say about junior colleges." And she said little that was affirmative. After all, a driving reason to write *could be* to complain, to expose bureaucratic incompetence and uncaring faculty. But, while there is some of that in the journal content, to complain is the over-riding concern of only two writers—the one discussed in this paragraph and for another African-American, a student at the same college.

The great majority of the writers took the opportunity to say something positive about their colleges and about their own lives. The students, especially, are excited about what is happening to them, about the changes that going back to school and experiencing success are bringing about. They are consciously enthusiastic about their prospects. They are able to feel they have some control over their lives, maybe for the first time in a long time, and they think they are going to follow certain steps and reach a goal. Why shouldn't they be happy to talk about it? Why wouldn't they want to encourage other women to follow them? College offers them more than just another chore; it offers exhilaration. The journal offered them a way to assert their own view of things, and through my study, to confront or persuade others of their worth.

A researcher who studies diaries wrote that for many women, "A personal diary, however limited its contents, is a way of asserting themselves as individuals; it says: 'What I set down is important. I am a subject in my own right, not just the object of others' thoughts or a convenience for them.'"[5] The writer thinks that even Filofaxers who report their days in brief snatches "are still saying subliminally, 'Some time each day belongs to me alone.' And now, when their roles have swelled to include all things endlessly, that's what women most need to say."

To Respond to a Particular "Asker"

For this category, there is little direct evidence in the journals themselves. I am relying more on the brief interviews I had with the writers when I first met them and on suggestions made more recently by women colleagues of mine.

For about half of the student writers, I was not the only person who asked them to participate in the study. I took most of their names from a list provided to me by a faculty member in the English Department. Sometimes that person asked the student beforehand if her name could be given to me so that I might contact her. The initial "asker," then, in these instances, may have been a valued (and usually former) teacher. In the case of the faculty writers, I wrote to each one directly without an intermediary, but I sometimes mentioned the name of the person I knew on their campus who had recommended them to me. I did this mostly to give myself some credibility,

---

[5] Harriet Blodgett, "Dear Diary: How Do I Need You? Let Me Count the Ways," *The New York Times Review of Books*, 22 September 1991, 1.

but the "recommender" might have been seen as someone to whom they would want to respond affirmatively.

I do not know exactly what happened in every case, but for the most part, I was the main "asker." In the case of five of the students, I know I was their only contact, since I simply walked up to them cold in the hall or the cafeteria and asked them to participate in the study. Whichever type of "asking" occurred, would another person have gotten a different return rate overall or an equal number of people who agreed to write?

A few seemed flattered to be asked by an ostensibly self-assured type wearing a suit. (Two student writers said so in later notes.) They may have felt complimented that someone sincerely wanted to know what they thought and felt. I have been told that I am believable and forceful, so that I appear "authentic." I know that I am passionate about my topic. I may have seemed the right person to get their ideas out to a wider public.

There were two questions that the women I approached had at first, both of which required trusting me. The students needed assurance that I would not be critical of their grammar or spelling (fear of ridicule), and the faculty wanted assurance of anonymity (fear of retaliation). Both groups appeared convinced enough by my promises to assume that I would keep my word.

Several of my colleagues have suggested that the writers responded to a woman asking a woman, but there is no direct evidence of this, and in my experience, many women respond just as readily when men ask favors. One could argue that women are even more likely to defer to men than to another woman. Whatever the case may be, the journals were written, ultimately, for a woman—for me. (And, of course, they wrote for themselves as well.) That may have influenced the content of their writing, if not their actual willingness to participate, and I have tried reading them with that in mind.

Karen McCarthy Brown, in an article in *The Chronicle of Higher Education*, discusses "writing about 'the other,' and new approaches to fieldwork that can end the colonial mindset of anthropological research."[6] Although I was a stranger to those I approached, I think that they were not "others" to me, nor I to them. I identify with both community college students and community college faculty, and that identification may have been apparent to the writers. While we probably will not become close friends, as did McCarthy Brown and the Haitian priestess that she studied, I am truly interested in their lives and look forward to sharing my results with them. I feel that I did not exploit them, nor misrepresent my intentions.

I think of the journal writers as colleagues. We are engaged in trying to pin down a particular phenomenon as coherently as we can. The task involves a reciprocal agreement. From my own point of view, the main reason they wrote the journals is the very same reason that I did the study. We believed we had something worth saying, and thus it was a cooperative venture: they were going to help me say it, and I was going to get it said for them.

Summary

In summary, there was a relative willingness to write the journals, more than might have been anticipated. Possible reasons for this fall into the following four categories:

---

[6] Karen McCarthy Brown, "Writing About 'The Other'," *The Chronicle of Higher Education*, 15 (April 1992): A56.

1. The writers tried to make sense of their own lives. Some were conscious of this intent before they wrote; others only discovered their greater understanding of themselves after they had written.

2. Some so-called traditional "feminine" personality traits were operating. Some of those who were asked wished to be "good girls," to be helpful and cooperative, and felt guilty if they did not perform up to their own expectations.

3. The writers had something they wanted to say that they thought was worth disseminating and thought that I would help them be heard. They wished to speak for themselves as a part of a larger community of women (and men) in the same situation.

4. Characteristics of those who asked them to write may have been persuasive.

Chapter 8

Conclusion

Do I contradict myself? Very well then I contradict myself.
(I am large, I contain multitudes.)

Walt Whitman, "Song of Myself"[1]

The overall contrast between the two images that I chose to compare seems clear from the summaries at the end of Chapters 3, 4, 5 and 6. Where the fictional re-entry woman student is often passive and sees the two-year college as a place where decisions will be made for her, the actual re-entry women students are actively involved in ordering their own lives and see the two-year college as a place that is helping them implement their plans. They may be incorrect in their assumptions, but this is the image that they have in their minds.

---

[1] Walt Whitman, "Song of Myself," in *The Works of Walt Whitman*, vol. 1 (New York: Funk and Wagnalls, 1968), 62-114.

The fictional student is usually living on the margins of society, but seldom questions the power structure that has placed her there, or even notices that there *is* a hierarchy of places in which she is situated toward the bottom. The actual student, on the other hand, resents the authoritarian arrangement that pushes her to the side and often organizes with others to fight on one front or another.

The joy of learning that surfaces in the writing of the two-year college students appears in a few fictional depictions, but with nowhere near the consistency that it emerges in the student journals. The difficulty that the re-entry woman has in juggling roles and schedules in order to attend college at all, even part time, is shown occasionally in fiction; the student journals are almost universal in discussing this theme and the stress that is associated with it.

A rare two-year college faculty member in fiction is a dedicated and competent teacher, nurturing students in a professional manner and striving to improve techniques, methodology, and an understanding of both students and subject matter. The journals of two-year college students and faculty depict such a teacher as one who can be found frequently in the actual classroom. The sense of mission and the cooperative spirit consistently expressed in the faculty journals are close to non-existent in fiction. In the fictional image, the two-year college is more likely to be a place containing bored and mediocre teachers.

Almost no fictional faculty see teaching as a significant career, nor is it seen as valuable by other characters. The journal-writing faculty, without exception, feel that what they and their colleagues are trying to do is clearly significant. For many of them, it is a serious "calling," followed with pride.

Students who are losers and faculty who are uninvolved exist in the real world. I do not argue that the fictional image can be found nowhere in the two-year college system of today. Thus, I began this chapter with the Whitman quote: the two-year colleges "contain multitudes." Most of these multitudes did not write journals for me. (Furthermore, why would any uncaring faculty member or witless student do so?)

My point in this study is that the very large number of people who are *not* uncaring or losers have been ignored or maligned by American culture for decades. To force everyone into the tidy little boxes created by fiction's stereotypes and then to dismiss them is to do an injustice to the great majority. Those connected to two-year colleges cannot help but internalize the stigma to some extent. (Isn't this one of the reasons that "The joy of learning I am intelligent" is so pronounced a theme among the student journal writers?)

The fictional image does not reflect actual demographics, since there are almost no minority students enrolled in fictional works. In actuality, large percentages of minority students in higher education begin at a community college. The journals of both faculty and students are quite aware of the racial and ethnic mix common to the American two-year college and comment on the strengths and the possible divisiveness it brings. The journal writers, especially the faculty writers, are very cognizant of racism, for instance, and many are active in combatting it in their own schools.

Despite their awareness and their sensitivity toward differences, neither the race or ethnicity of the faculty writer nor the identity or location of the college she is writing about are discernable to a reader. The same problems and the same vitality are present in every one of the five colleges from which I drew the journal writers. I tested out this phenomenon, on a casual basis, by having several different readers, insiders *and* outsiders to the two-year college system, read passages from the journals that appear in this book and then try to guess the race, the ethnicity, or the geographic location of the person who wrote it. Even those readers who were sure they could accomplish this task easily did no better than chance.

Why do I mention this? For one thing, it is a piece of evidence that the actual two-year college inhabitants have much in common, and I believe that if they (we) unite, we might counteract the continually pejorative image bestowed upon us by our detractors. In addition, this could be done without denying the actual faults and problems of the colleges, thus losing our chance to correct them. The same strengths, the same faults, and the same problems appear across the board, though perhaps more profoundly in some places than in others. The two-year colleges might "rise up," both in image and in actuality, by working together.

The Demeaning Image of the "Twos" v. The Satirical Image of the "Fours"

It has been pointed out to me more than once that American fiction, including that of popular culture, *usually* depicts the four-year colleges and universities in a satirical or mocking way.[2] The absent-minded or the overly-ambitious professor and the hedonistic or the materialistic student are stock characters in many novels and movies. Therefore, how are the two-year colleges treated differently from higher

---

[2] Before I even started this study, Wayne Booth, Department of English at the University of Chicago, questioned me on this issue. When I thought I was finished with the study, Amy Rose, Department of Leadership and Educational Policy Studies at Northern Illinois University, questioned me again. And several people in between these two posed the same objection. Therefore, I felt that I needed to spend some time addressing the question.

education in general? Except for the profound invisibility of the two-year college, isn't this the same phenomenon? (The significance of the invisibility is always granted by everyone, and I will discuss that aspect of the demeaning image or non-image later in this chapter.)

There are several ways to counter the assertion that *all* higher education is treated pejoratively and that thus the community college is not a special case.

1. "Going to college" or "graduating from the university" has never been a low-status marker in American culture. It has never been used as shorthand for "loser," as Chapter 2 on the single-mention list argues has occurred for the two-year college. And when "going to college" is treated at length in fiction, the image is not an indication of the low intelligence or ability of all who are involved in higher education. This is true no matter how negative or mocking the fictional image of the college or university depicted.

2. Almost always in fiction, it is considered a "good thing" to go to college. It is a step up, or at least not a step in the wrong direction. It is certainly not an action one might be embarrassed to have made public, or to put on one's vita, however sturdy the anti-intellectual strain may be in the United States. Fictional characters announce that their children are in college without hesitation, indeed with pride. And there is a certain vanity in being depicted as even the most animal-like of students or bumbling of professors, as long as the students or faculty are in four-year colleges—especially *prestigious* colleges.[3]

There are no prestigious two-year colleges in fiction. In fact, very few distinctions are made of any kind among

---

[3] It has been estimated by those who study the college novel that more than three-quarters of them are set in one of two schools—Harvard and Yale.

two-year schools. There is an underlying assumption made in fiction that they are all the same. This belief in sameness is never applied to the four-year schools, where a well-known and fairly rigid hierarchy exists.

3. It is true that fiction about four-year colleges is often comic in tone. Much of the humor centers around pretentious faculty mis-teaching thoughtless students. Especially when the college in question is Ivy League (and it most often is), the entertainment for the reader or viewer is connected to a kind of envy of those who are detached from the "real" world, without the responsibility and accountability that others must bear. There is sometimes even an oblique fondness for the idiosyncracies that detachment from "reality" fosters.

No one envies a two-year college character. No one is fondly nostalgic, in fiction, for the care-free, fun-filled days of higher education at a community college. For most writers of fiction, to put "community" and "college" together is to create an oxymoron. To spend one's life on a two-year college faculty is to be condemned to the abyss. To spend a lifetime at a university is at least an enviable sinecure.

4. To quote Molly Ivins in a review of a humorous book, "Satire is a weapon of the powerless against the powerful. When satire is aimed at powerless people, it is not only cruel but profoundly vulgar."[4] The Saturday Night Live "Community College Bowl" skit is an example of the profoundly vulgar, as is Edward Mackin's depiction of urban minorities in *The Nominative Case*. The college novel set at Harvard or Yale is hardly poking fun at the marginal, but taking on, and usually at the same time allying itself with, the wealthy and

---

[4] Molly Ivins, in a review of Joe Queenan, *Imperial Caddy: The Rise of Dan Quayle in America and the Decline and Fall of Practically Everything Else*, *The New York Times Review of Books*, 11 October 1992, 9.

the powerful. The popularity of the film *Animal House* only increased applications to Dartmouth, the Ivy League college that provided its setting.[5] But it is quite unlikely that people who have a community college as their only option will be encouraged to enroll by the mean-spirited images that fiction most often provides.

5. As I collected examples of two-year college characters in fiction from many correspondents, there were a few mis-directed leads, as one might expect; i.e., leads to fictional works where the characters were connected to other kinds of schools or colleges, including four-year schools. Each mis-direction led me to low-status and poorly informed students at mediocre schools. Usually the students were re-entry women, as well. In other words, my correspondents mis-re-membered their reading or viewing, with the thought that if it was about the ignorant lower classes or about re-entry women, it must take place in a community college.

I believe that this mis-direction makes the point for my argument. That is, satirical depictions of higher education mock different aspects of the "fours" than the "twos." The two-year colleges are demeaned for their marginal inhabi-tants, so much so that when such a devalued and "declassed" image of higher education appears, its audience assumes that the college in question is not a four-year school.

6. Although I found more than fifty examples of the two-year college in fiction, very few of them inform their audience, correctly or otherwise, of what activities might go on at such a place. Works about four-year colleges are not only vastly greater in number, but actually depict the college and its operation in some way.

---

[5] *National Lampoon's Animal House*, directed by John Landis, 1978, motion picture.

That is, in most works about two-year colleges, even those that are not on the single-mention list, "junior college" and "community college" are simply low-status markers, negative filters through which all other information must pass. For example, I treated Garrison Keillor's *WLT: A Radio Romance* at some length, but the two-year college was mentioned specifically only once, at the beginning of Professor Shell's dismal episode. It was meant to be comically belittling—one more way of indicating to the reader the character's status as a joke professor. His students, who are also mentioned only once, are jokes as well. They do not even seem like probable two-year college students, since "the semester ended and they all went home," an event which is more likely to happen at a resident four-year college.

Keillor could not have used "a *university* in New Hampshire" as his negative filter. "University" would simply have been another piece of information, no more or less belittling than "New Hampshire." "A junior college in New Hampshire" indicates, in Keillor's context, that the institution, its faculty, and its students are not to be taken seriously.

7. Finally, we can take the fictional image a step further than ridicule into other kinds of punishment. Fictional students in two-year colleges are mostly women. This is not true of four-year college fictional students, who are still mostly male. (In reality, slightly more than one-half of all four-year college undergraduates are now female, but fiction and mythology have not yet caught up with this fact.) As Carolyn Heilbrun, the feminist writer formerly at Columbia University, says, "In life, as in fiction, women who speak out usually end up punished or dead."[6] I won't argue about life, but we

---

[6] Carolyn Heilbrun, quoted by Anne Matthews, "Rage in a Tenured Position," *The New York Times Magazine*, 8 November 1992, 47.

saw in Chapter 3 that most re-entry women students (and two-year college women faculty) are punished severely for their presumption in trying to gain some control of their lives.[7]

It must be a very small minority of fictional men students who are punished for figuratively "speaking out of turn" simply by attending college. Since, in traditional mythology, their behavior is not "out of turn" at all, but admirable, it need not be punished. Are the re-entry students punished and belittled because they are women, or punished because they are at a two-year college? The two categories may be inseparable in the minds of some writers.

Invisibility

> The worst sin towards our fellow creatures is not to hate them, but to be indifferent to them. That is the essence of inhumanity.
>
> George Bernard Shaw, *The Devil's Disciple*[8]

There is another pair of categories that may be inseparable: the cheerless image of the two-year college, on the one hand, and its even more widespread invisibility, on the other. It is logical that what is considered not worth noticing will be viewed negatively when it makes an occasional appearance.

What is it about the two-year college system that makes it microscopic in cultural visibility even though it is huge in size? What is it about this large, long-lived creature that

---

[7] More women than men suffer afflictions, medical and otherwise, in television fiction, according to Susan Gunderson, "In My Opinion," *The Portland Oregonian*, 28 May 1991, B7. Is the fictional two-year college just another way to show women as victims?

[8] George Bernard Shaw, *The Devil's Disciple*, Act II (New York: Penguin Books, 1976), 35.

prevents people from seeing it? To whose benefit is it that it remains unnoticed? Visibility is a question of power; those who determine visibility are dominant, and the invisible are, by definition, unsubstantial.

Even people who spend their working lives in two-year colleges have difficulty remembering a single fictional character, even in a movie or on television, who is connected to such an institution, although they can recall the character when reminded of a particular instance. When an established part of society as pervasive and as heavily populated as the two-year college remains invisible even to those who are its inhabitants, there must be an element of pretense involved. There must be an intentionality of some kind. Why is this phenomenon so characteristic?

The four-year schools set the pattern for what it means to be a college student or teacher. Stigmatized inhabitants of the two-year schools confront a society that has long been oriented to the four-year model. In American mythology, the typical college student is in the process of late adolescent development. He (or, less often, she) is about eighteen or so, a full-time student, and living on the campus of a four-year college or university. According to Arthur Cohen, this very traditional image misses the great majority of today's college students, but persists nonetheless.[9]

Thus, the community college does not fit either the popular or the elite image, and so is seldom seen, or belittled as a "misfit" when noticed. The fact that the American student body at all levels of higher education has changed drastically in the past few decades has gone largely unrecognized by the general culture. In some ways, the four-year schools them-

---

[9] Arthur Cohen, in a conversation in Chicago, 2 May 1992.

selves have been especially blind and slow in accommodating the "non-traditional" students who comprise the fastest-growing groups. Our culture needs to unlearn some "facts," and our fiction could help it to do so.

In part, the myth of the "traditional student" is like the legendary American president who was born in a log cabin. Few presidents ever were, and certainly none were in the twentieth century, but still today candidates for the office, even patricians like George Bush, try to get as close to the myth as they can in their advertised images. A second, and maybe better, example of invisibility conferred by the powerful might be that of the image of African-Americans in advertisements of the 1950s. They were almost 100 percent invisible, even when servants or others in menial positions were depicted in magazines like *House Beautiful* or *Home and Garden*. In order for advertising to appeal to the major consumers, large numbers of low-status people were kept out of the way, "invisibilized" out of existence. Or, in a third example, attending a two-year college may be like housework and other ordinary things done by women: absolutely necessary, but generally invisible, except when manufacturers are trying to sell cleaning products to those who do the work.

It is easy enough to infer why those in positions of power, along with those whose task it is to reflect their views back to our culture, choose to ignore re-entry women and other inhabitants of two-year colleges. The more interesting question, for me, is why so many of the inhabitants themselves comply in their own invisibility and denigration. Several of the student journal writers report that they once held to the "official" view, but they changed their minds after experiencing an actual two-year college. Why don't more administrators and faculty draw on what they know to be positive in order to gain a more balanced view? They, after all, are usually more experienced than the students. Or, why don't the many writers on two-year college faculties at least draw on what they know to be *negative*, and thus counteract some of the invisibility? There are published novelists, for instance, who have taught full time at a two-year college for decades and never once use any background from that part of their lives when they write.

There is a quality of denial present in this phenomenon. Marge Piercy, the novelist and poet, has a community college reference in one of her books, so I wrote my usual letter asking if she knew of any other examples. She wrote back, "I'm afraid I can't help you . . . Only someone with a special sensitivity to that subject could remember such references."[10] Her reply was a little dismissive, I thought, but unfortunately true. Truer than she knows, perhaps, since most community college "insiders" themselves apparently lack that sensitivity.

Ask almost any African-American on a two-year college faculty about the treatment or presence of African-Americans on fictional television or in movies or literature, and you will get an immediate answer and maybe even a good analysis. Even those who are not "specially sensitized" to African-American culture will agree with Camille Cosby's doctoral research that found that blacks are often negatively portrayed on television as excitable and associated with drugs and violence, with the depreciated images often disguised as "humor."[11] The same immediate response and analysis will be forthcoming when most women faculty are asked about fictional women characters. They can remember many exam-

---

[10]Marge Piercy, unpublished letter to Nancy LaPaglia, 11 May 1992.

[11]Camille Cosby, "The Influence of Television Imagery on Selected African-American Young Adults' Self-Perceptions" (Ph.D. diss., University of Massachusetts, 1992).

ples without hesitation and give an analysis of their treatment in our culture. But ask community college faculty of any race or either gender about two-year college characters in fiction? In the vast majority of cases, they will come up blank.

In fact, most of the leads I got to two-year college characters came from college *administrators*, even though I sent my questionnaires mainly to faculty and to writers. I can only speculate as to the causes of this blind spot. It might make an interesting research question for another writer.

Future Possibilities

My original intent was to make the invisible more visible and the unfairly maligned more valued by their detractors. Has this study succeeded in any way or will it be successful in the future? There are a few possibilities.

During the course of my research, I wrote to and spoke with many authors, especially those who are currently connected to a two-year college. My purpose was to discuss their work and to ask for further leads, but I had an underlying "wish" agenda as well. Perhaps, I thought, just raising my questions will encourage them to consider two-year college characters differently. The feminists, at least, should be writing about such schools, either for their successes or for their failed promises. There is drama in the lives of community college inhabitants that can be explored by writers in all media.

In answer to my inquiry, for example, Tom Wolfe wrote back that his current novel-in-progress has such a character, a man who went to a community college in Contra Costa County, California. "What synchronicity, as Jung used to say," wrote Wolfe, that he was writing about him when my letter arrived.[12] I can at least daydream that Wolfe will give the character an extra line, or even make him a more rounded person, because of our correspondence. Other writers who are connected to a community college told me they would write a story set in their school in the future. I hope that they will do so.

Since I continue to collect fictional examples and write to each author, this process will continue. I already have many more examples than I cover in this study, since in June of 1992 I stopped rewriting chapters for the purpose of including new leads. I have heard of and from other authors since then. Some, like Texan Bill Crider, are community college faculty members who are not blind to their own situations. Others should not acquiesce in what they know is a one-sided image of a more complex situation or be fearful that outsiders will connect them to their low-status jobs if they write about them.

The use of journals can be especially rewarding.Besides providing data, they brought an extra bonus to me, and can do the same for other community college faculty. Just as L. Glenn Smith said that writing about Pestalozzi, the educator, helped him understand himself and not just his subject,[13] so the autobiographies I collected and analyzed helped me understand my own role in the community college, both as a former student and as a faculty member of long standing. Two-year college fiction, at present, never has the same effect. I hope that it will offer a fuller picture at some future time, since it is generally acknowledged that literature can—and should—help us to perceive ourselves with greater clarity.

---

[12]Tom Wolfe, unpublished letter to Nancy LaPaglia, 11 February 1992.

[13]L. Glenn Smith, *Self-Disclosure, Externalization, and Projection: Biography as Personal Discovery*, 1989 Illinois Society of Educational Biographers presidential address.

The faculty journal writers, though they do not know each other, formed a group united in defense of a common cause. They are united, for the most part, both against their powerful detractors and against the purists who use elite colleges as the only model for higher education. Many of the student journal writers joined their teachers in counteracting the negative image.

"Diary-keeping has been a female experience that has often kept us closeted writers," says bell hooks in "Writing from the Darkness."[14] "Diary writing has not been traditionally seen by literary scholars as subversive autobiography that challenges the conventional notions of it as mere documentation." In many cases, she adds, this writing enables women to experience self-definition, self-discovery, and self-recovery.

Reading the journals over again makes me think that some of this self-definition happened to the autobiographers who were my partners in this project, and I hope that it will happen to those who read their journal excerpts in this book. I thank, once again, the thirty-seven women who came along with me on a voyage of discovery.

---

[14] bell hooks, "Writing From the Darkness," *Tri-Quarterly* (Spring-Summer 1989): 72.

Sources Consulted

Amstutz, Donna. "The Silenced Partners: A Study of Unacknowledged Mentoring by Secretaries." Ed.D. diss., Northern Illinois University, 1989.

Barthelme, Donald. *Paradise*. New York: Putnam, 1986.

_____. "Lightning." In *Forty Stories*. New York: Penguin Books, 1987, 172-80.

Beile, Walter. "The Fat Plumber." *The Wright Side* (April 1992): 12-14.

Bellow, Saul. *The Adventures of Augie March*. New York: Viking, 1953.

Berger, Peter L., and Thomas Luckmann. *The Social Construction of Reality: A Treatise in the Sociology of Knowledge*. New York: Doubleday, 1967.

Blodgett, Harriet. "Dear Diary: How Do I Need You? Let Me Count the Ways." *The New York Times Review of Books*, 22 September 1991.

The Bonfire of the Vanities. Directed and produced by Brian DePalma, 1990. Motion picture.

Brent, Stephen, and Jerome Karabel. *The Diverted Dream: Unfulfilled Promises of the Community College, 1904-85*. Oxford, England: Oxford University Press, 1989.

Brown, Karen McCarthy. "Writing About 'The Other'." *The Chronicle of Higher Education* (15 April 1992): A56.

Bryant, Dorothy. *Ella Price's Journal*. Berkeley, CA: ATA Books, 1972.

Bull Durham. Directed by Ron Shelton, 1988. Motion picture.

Carlyle, Thomas. "On History." *In Critical and Miscellaneous Essays*. London: J. Fraser, 1839.

Chamberlin, W. J. S. *Toward a Phenomenology of Education*.
    Philadelphia: Westminster Press, 1969.
"Cheers." 1991. Television series.
The Chronicle of Higher Education Abstracts. Chicago:
    University of Chicago Press, 1991.
Clark, Burton. "The Cooling Out Function Revisited." Chap. in
    Questioning the Community College Role. New Directions
    for Community Colleges Series, no. 32. San Francisco:
    Jossey-Bass, 1980, 15-31.
Cohen, Arthur, and Florence Brawer. *The Collegiate Function of
    Community Colleges*. San Francisco: Jossey-Bass, 1987.
Constantine, K. C. *The Man Who Liked Slow Tomatoes*. Boston:
    David R. Godine Publishing, 1982.
Corrin, Dean. *Butler County*. Victory Gardens Theatre, Chicago,
    1984.
Cosby Camille. "The Influence of Television Imagery on
    Selected African-American Young Adults." Ph.D. diss.,
    University of Massachusetts, 1992.
Coughlin, T. Glen. *The Hero of New York*. New York: Norton,
    1986.
Crider, Bill. *Shotgun Saturday Night*. New York: Walker &
    Company, 1987.
_____. *Blood Marks*. New York: St. Martin's Press, 1991.
_____. *Dead on the Island*. New York: Walker & Company,
    1991.
Csikszentmihalyi, Mihaly. *Flow: The Psychology of Optimal
    Experience*. New York: Harper & Row, 1990.
Cunningham, Phyllis. "Own Your Advocacy." *Adult Learning
    Magazine*, November 1990.
Dillard, Annie. *Living by Fiction*. New York: Harper & Row,
    1982.
_____. *The Writing Life*. New York: Harper & Row, 1989.
Dobberstein, Keith. "The Evolution of the City Colleges of
    Chicago." Paper presented at the Seventh Annual Illinois
    History Symposium, Springfield, IL, 5 December 1986.

Duneier, Mitchell. *Slim's Table: Race, Respectability, and Masculinity*. Chicago: University of Chicago Press, 1992.

Edgerton, Clyde. *Raney*. Chapel Hill, NC: Algonquin Books, 1985.

Eisenstadt, Jill. *From Rockaway*. New York: Alfred Knopf, 1987.

French, Marilyn. *The Women's Room*. New York: Simon & Schuster, 1977.

Frye, Northrop. *Anatomy of Criticism: Four Essays*. Princeton: Princeton University Press, 1957.

"Gimme a Break!" 1991. Television series.

Glass, J. Conrad, and Anita Rose. "Re-entry Women: A Growing and Unique College Population." *NASPA Journal* 25, no. 2 (Fall 1987): 110-19.

Gobledale, Ana K. "The Learning Spirit: The Spirituality of Adult Education." Ed.D. diss., Northern Illinois University, 1991.

Grattan, C. H. *In Quest for Knowledge*. New York: Association Press, 1955.

Griffiths, Trevor. *Comedians*. New York: Grove Press, 1976.

_____. With additional dialogue and rewriting by Aaron Freeman. *Comedians*. Court Theatre, Chicago, April 1992.

Gunderson, Susan. "In My Opinion." *The Oregonian*, 28 May 1991.

Hall, Donald. "Six Poets in Search of a Lawyer." In *Exiles and Marriages*. New York: Viking, 1955, 61-62.

Hart, Carolyn. *A Little Class on Murder*. New York: Bantam, 1989.

Heilbrun, Carolyn. "Rage in a Tenured Position." Interview by Anne Matthews. *The New York Times Magazine*, 8 November 1992.

Hess, Joan. *Strangled Prose*. New York: Ballantine, 1986.

Hill, Elizabeth. "Literary Research and the Study of Re-Entry Women." *Continuing Higher Education* 37, no. 2 (Spring 1989): 7-10.

Hill, Elizabeth. "A Study of Re-entry Women in Fiction and Research: A Comparative Analysis." Ph.D. diss., University of Iowa, 1990.

hooks, bell. "Writing From the Darkness." *Tri-Quarterly* (Spring-Summer, 1989): 71-77.

Huston, Aletha, et al. *Big World, Small Screen: The Role of Television in American Society.* Lincoln, NE: University of Nebraska Press, 1992.

Inge, William. *Good Luck, Miss Wyckoff.* Boston: Little, Brown, 1970.

Ivins, Molly. Review of *Imperial Caddy: The Rise of Dan Quayle in America and the Decline and Fall of Practically Everything Else,* by Joe Queenan. In *The New York Times Review of Books,* 11 October 1992.

Jencks, Christopher. *Inequality: A Reassessment of the Effect of Family and Schooling in America.* New York: Basic Books, 1972.

Jones, R. D. "The Deer Leg Chronicle." *Southern Magazine,* February 1989, 46, 56-57.

Kaye, Elizabeth. "What I Think of Other Women." *Esquire,* August 1992, 94-104.

Keillor, Garrison. *WLT: A Radio Romance.* New York: Viking, 1991.

King, Stephen. *The Stand.* New York: Doubleday, 1990.

Kramer, John E., Jr. *The American College Novel.* New York: Garland, 1981.

LaPaglia, Nancy. "The Missing Majority: The Community College in American Fiction." In *Model Voices: Finding a Writing Voice,* ed. Jeffrey Sommers. New York: McGraw-Hill, 1989, 442-49.

Leffland, Ella. "Last Courtesies." In *Last Courtesies and Other Stories.* New York: Harper & Row, 1980.

Lyons, John O. *The College Novel in America.* Carbondale, IL: Southern Illinois University Press, 1962.

Mackin, Edward. *The Nominative Case.* New York: Walker & Company, 1991.

Maid to Order. Directed and Produced by Carl Reiner and Liz Glotzer, 1987. Motion picture.

Mann, Sylvia. "Complementarity, Dissonance and Awakening: Major Themes in the Career Lives of Women in Traditional Occupations." Ed.D. diss., Northern Illinois University, 1991.

"The Mary Tyler Moore Show." Television series, 1990.

Mason, Bobbie Ann. "Shiloh." In *Shiloh and Other Stories*. New York: Harper & Row, 1982.

Merriam, Sharan. *Themes of Adulthood Through Literature*. New York: Teachers College Press, Columbia University, 1983.

Miami Blues. Directed and produced by Jonathan Demme and Gary Goetzman, 1990. Motion picture.

Millman, Nancy. "Crash Course." *Chicago*, September 1992, 110-13, 132-34.

Miner, Valerie. *Murder in the English Department*. New York: St. Martin's Press, 1982.

Moore, Lorrie. *Anagrams*. New York: Alfred Knopf, 1986.

Morrison, Toni, ed. *Race-ing Justice, En-gendering Power: Essays on Anita Hill, Clarence Thomas, and the Construction of Social Reality*. New York: Pantheon, 1992.

National Lampoon's Animal House. Directed by John Landis, 1978. Motion picture.

Naylor, Gloria. *The Women of Brewster Place*. New York: Penguin Books, 1982.

"Night Court." Fall 1991. Television series.

Nobody's Child. Directed by Lee Grant, 1986. Made-for-TV motion picture.

El Norte. Directed and produced by Gregory Nava and Anna Thomas, 1983. Motion picture.

Oates, Joyce Carol. *Them*. New York: Ballantine, 1969.

_____. "Angst." In *The Hungry Ghosts*. Los Angeles: Black Sparrow Press, 1975, 181-200.

Ohliger, John. *The Fictional Adult Educator*. Springfield, IL: Basic Choices, 1989.

Orfield, Gary. *Toward a Strategy of Urban Integration: Lessons in School and Housing Policy from Twelve Cities: A Report to the Ford Foundation.* New York: Ford Foundation, 1981.

_____. *The Chicago Study of Access and Choice in Higher Education: A Report to the Illinois Senate Committee on Higher Education.* Chicago: University of Chicago Press, Committee on Public Policy Studies Research Project, 1984.

The Oxford English Dictionary. Oxford, England: Oxford University Press, 1971.

Pascarella, Ernest, and Patrick Terenzini. *How College Affects Students: Findings and Insights from Twenty Years of Research.* San Francisco: Jossey-Bass, 1991.

Pelletier, Nancy. *The Rearrangement.* New York: Macmillan, 1985.

Pittman, Von, and John Theilmann. "The Administrator in Fiction: Portrayals of Higher Education." *Educational Forum* 50, no. 4 (Summer 1986): 405-18.

Plato. *The Republic.* Translated by Desmond Lee. New York: Penguin Books, 1955.

Polkinghorne, Donald. *Narrative Knowing and the Human Sciences.* Albany, NY: State University of New York Press, 1988.

"Pottery Will Get You Nowhere." In "The Wonder Years." January 1989. Television series.

Quigley, Alan. "The Resisters: An Analysis of Non-Participation in Adult Basic Education." Ed.D. diss., Northern Illinois University, 1987.

Raleigh, Michael. *Death in Uptown.* New York: St. Martin's Press, 1991.

"Reasonable Doubts." 1992. Television series.

Robinson, Rhonda. "How Can You 'Know' if You Can't Control? New Research Issues in Instructional Technology." Paper presented at the fifth annual LEPS Department awards convocation, Northern Illinois University, October 1991.

"Room for Two." 22 April 1992. Television series.

Rosten, Leo. *The Education of H*Y*M*A*N K*A*P*L*A*N.* New York: Harcourt Brace, 1937.

Russell, Bertrand. *The Conquest of Happiness.* New York: Liveright Publishing, 1930.

Salinger, J. D. *The Catcher in the Rye.* New York: Little, Brown, 1945.

Sanderson, Jim. "Stripping." *Ellipsis* 1, no. 3 (Campbell, CA: Ellipsis Press, 1989).

"Saturday Night Live." 5 October 1991. Television series.

Schaeffer, Susan Fromberg. *Falling.* New York: Macmillan, 1973.

Schlachter, Stephany S. "Education for Older Adults: An Analysis of National Public Policy." Ed.D. diss., Northern Illinois University, 1991.

Shaw, George Bernard. *The Devil's Disciple,* Act II. New York: Penguin Books, 1976.

Sibling Rivalry. Directed and produced by Carl Reiner and Liz Glotzer, 1990. Motion picture.

Siefert, Lynn. *Little Egypt.* Steppenwolf Theatre, Chicago, December 1987.

"The Simpsons." April 1991. Television series.

Smith, L. Glenn. "Self-Disclosure, Externalization, and Projection: Biography as Personal Discovery." Presidential address given to the Illinois Society of Educational Biographers, 1989.

Smith, Lee. *Oral History.* New York: Putnam, 1983.

_____. "Bob, A Dog." In *Me and My Baby View the Universe.* New York: Ballantine, 1990.

Smith, Page. *Killing the Spirit: Higher Education in America.* New York: Penguin Books, 1990.

Spinelli, Jerry. *Space Station Seventh Grade.* Boston: Little, Brown, 1982.

Stanage, Sherman. Adult Education and Phenomenological Research. Malabar, FL: Krieger Publishing, 1987.

Starting Over. Directed by Alan J. Pukula, 1979. Motion picture.

Stegner, Wallace. Where the Bluebird Sings to the Lemonade Springs: Living and Writing in the West. New York: Random House, 1992.

Steinem, Gloria. Revolution from Within: A Book of Self-Esteem. Boston: Little, Brown, 1992.

Sternberg, Alan. "Moose." The New Yorker, 12 September 1988.

Steward, David, and Algis Mickunas. Exploring Phenomenology: A Guide to the Field and Its Literature. 2d ed. Athens, OH: Ohio University Press, 1990.

Tannen, Deborah. You Just Don't Understand: Women and Men in Conversation. New York: Morrow, 1990.

Thelin, John, and Barbara Townsend. "Fiction to Fact: College Novels and the Study of Higher Education." In Higher Education: Handbook of Theory and Research IV. New York: Agathon Press, 1988.

Thelma and Louise. Directed by Ridley Scott, 1991. Motion picture.

"Thirtysomething." 1991. Television series.

Throw Mama From the Train. Directed and produced by Danny DeVito and Larry Brezner, 1990. Motion picture.

Tolstoi, Leo. "The Death of Ivan Ilych." In The Short Novels of Tolstoi. New York: Dial Press, 1946. 409-70.

Vandermeer, Barbara. "The Academic Novel as a Resource in the Study of Higher Education." Ph.D. diss., University of Alabama, 1982.

Vaughan, George B. The Community College in America. Washington, DC: Community College Press, 1985.

Wagner, Jane. The Search for Signs of Intelligent Life in the Universe. New York: Harper & Row, 1986.

Wakefield, Dan. Starting Over. New York: Delacorte Press, 1983.

Walker, Walter. The Immediate Prospect of Being Hanged. New York: Viking, 1989.

Whitman, Walt. "Song of Myself." In The Works of Walt Whitman, vol. 1. New York: Funk and Wagnalls, 1968, 62-114.

Willeford, Charles. *The Burnt Orange Heresy*. New York: Crown
     Publications, 1971.
_____. *Miami Blues*. New York: Ballantine, 1984.
Williams, Tennessee. *The Glass Menagerie*. New York: New
     Directions, 1945.
Wilson, J. J. "Books That Changed Our Lives." *Women's Studies
     Quarterly* 19, nos. 3 and 4 (Fall/Winter 1991): 8-29.
Wilson, Michael, scriptwriter. *Salt of the Earth*. Old Westbury,
     NY: Feminist Press, 1978.
Wolfe, Tom. *The Bonfire of the Vanities*. New York: Farrar,
     Straus, 1987.
"The Wonder Years." 1991. Television series.
Wong, Jade Snow. *Fifth Chinese Daughter*. New York: Harper &
     Row, 1945.
_____. *Fifth Chinese Daughter*. New York: Harper & Row,
     1945; reprint, Seattle, WA: University of Washington Press,
     1989.
Woolf, Virginia. *The Years*. New York: Harcourt, Brace, 1937.

Index

A

Adjunct faculty. *See* part-time faculty
Administration, two-year college, 115-16, 127, 157
The Adventures of Augie March, 33-4
African-Americans. *See also* minorities
    faculty in fiction, 91
    journal writers, 61, 68, 108, 139
    stereotypes in fiction, 13-14, 156
    students, 12
    students in fiction, 27, 34, 38, 45, 53, 54
Agency, sense of
    in fiction, 65
    in student journals, 64, 66-71, 85
    in women, *xviii*
Alcoholism and other addictions, in fiction, 91
Anagrams, 98
"Angst," 98-99
Animal House, National Lampoon's, 151
Autobiography, 15, 18, 117, 158. *See also* journals

B

Barthelme, Donald, 23, 24
Beile, Walter, 54-55, 92
Bellow, Saul, 33-34
Blood Marks, 96

"Bob, a Dog," 25
The Bonfire of the Vanities, 27
"Books That Changed Our Lives," 41-42
Booth, Wayne, *xviii*, 148
Brent, Stephen and Jerome Karabel, 11, 36
Brown, Karen McCarthy, 142
Bryant, Dorothy, 29, 38-39, 41-42, 101-02
Butler County, 46
The Burnt Orange Heresy, 27

C

Careers, of journal writers, 62, 63-64, 146
"Cheers," 28
Children and families
    in faculty journals, 108
    in fiction, 39, 45, 70-71, 96
    in student journals, 60, 61, 62, 66, 70-71, 72, 73, 77, 81,
        86, 87
City Colleges of Chicago, 12, 33, 42, 53-54, 59, 66, 74, 86,
        91, 94
Clark, Burton, 11, 102
Cohen, Arthur, 12, 63, 154
Colleges, four-year, and universities
    compared to two-year colleges, 11, 116
    image, 148-153
    in fiction, 28
Comedians, 53-54, 91
Community colleges. *See* two-year colleges
The Conquest of Happiness, *xiv*
Constantine, K. C., 43
Conway, Jill Ker, *xviii*, 117
"Cooling-out" theory, 11, 102

Cooperative actions among women, 78, 118-19, 138, 142, 146
Corrin, Dean, 46
Cosby, Camille, 156
Coughlin, T. Glen, 46, 98
Crider, Bill, 30, 52-53, 96, 158
Cunningham, Phyllis, 16

D

Daley College, 59, 74. *See also* City Colleges of Chicago
Dead on the Island, 52-53
Death in Uptown, 30
"The Deer-Leg Chronicle," 25
Dillard, Annie, 13, 17, 124
The Diverted Dream, 36
Dumping ground, two-year colleges as a, 122, 125, 126-7, 128
Duneier, Mitchell, 13-14
Bull Durham, 95

E

Early retirement, 107
Edgerton, Clyde, 47-48, 97
Eisenstadt, Jill, 24
Ella Price's Journal, 29, 38-39, 41, 101-02
English as a Second Language (ESL), 10, 111
English teachers in two-year colleges
    in actuality, 30, 52
    in fiction, 26, 32, 37, 47, 93, 95, 97, 98, 99, 100-03

F

Faculty women, definition, 10
Falling, 42, 94
Families. *See* children and families
"The Fat Plumber," 54-55, 92
Feminism, *xvii-xviii*, 21-22, 157-57
      in fiction, 27, 39-40, 42, 44, 45, 152
      in the journals, 124, 138
Fiction
      definition, 9
      as a reflection of society, 17
Fifth Chinese Daughter, 34-36, 92
Freeman, Aaron, 53-54, 91
French, Marilyn, 95-96
From Rockaway, 24

G

G.E.D. exam, 9, 10, 59, 66, 111
Good Luck, Miss Wyckoff, 38
Griffiths, Trevor, 53-54, 91

H

Hall, Donald, 26
Harold Washington College, 59. *See also* City Colleges of
          Chicago
Hart, Carolyn, 26
The Hero of New York, 46, 98
Hess, Joan, 27
Hill, Elizabeth, 17
hooks, bell, 159

I

Image, definition, 8
The Immediate Prospect of Being Hanged, 24
"The Influence of Television Imagery on Selected African-
          American Young Adults," 156
Inge, William, 38
Insider
          definition, 8
          journal writers, 58, 75
Interviews
          of journal writers, 20, 77, 79
          as a methodology, 15
Invisibility of two-year colleges, 2-3, 15, 35, 149, 153-57

J

Jones, R. D., 25
Journal
          definition, 10, 58
          the experience of writing, 65
          in fiction, 38, 101
          as a methodology, 15, 58
          response from writers, 131-32, 136-37
          return rate, 59, 132
          themes, 132-142
Journal writers
          faculty demographics, 107-09
          faculty who started at two-year colleges, 110-17
          student demographics, 58-64
Joy of learning
          definition, 80
          "joy of learning I am intelligent," 80-84, 147

        lack of joy, 80
        theme in journals, 19, 64, 79-84, 127, 146
Juggling, 64, 84-87, 146
Junior colleges. *See* two-year colleges.

K

Keillor, Garrrison, 102-03, 152
Killing the Spirit, 89-90
King, Stephen, 42, 92-93

L

"Last Courtesies," 25
Leffland, Ella, 25
A Little Class on Murder, 26
Little Egypt, 25
Living by Fiction, 13, 17

M

Mackin, Edward, 29, 53, 100-01, 150
Maid to Order, 27
Male students in fiction, 46, 92, 152
The Man Who Liked Slow Tomatoes, 43
Mann, Sylvia, 109
Marginality as a theme, 19, 29, 64, 72-79, 116, 121-25,
        146, 151
"The Mary Tyler Moore Show," 98
Mason, Bobbie Ann, *xviii*, 1-3, 43, 65, 72, 79, 84
McInerney, Ralph. *See* Edward Mackin
Methodology
        analysis of documents, 20

fiction, the use of, 15, 16
   intended audience, 21-22
   journals, the use of, 18-19, 67, 76, 140-41
   research questions asked and not asked, 6-7, 11-13
   storytellers, 14
Miami Blues, 27, 44, 100
Miner, Valerie, 26
Minorities, 61, 68, 72, 111 *See also* African-Americans
   faculty, 108, 123
   faculty in fiction, 54
   students, 54, 86, 126, 147
   students in fiction, 7, 24, 34, 38, 53, 54, 76-77, 92
Mission, a sense of, 105, 109, 115, 116-17, 117-19, 127,
      146
Mohawk Valley Community College, 59. *See also* two-year
      colleges
Moore, Laurie, 98
"Moose," 25
Multi-cultural, 11, 34, 50, 91
Murder in the English Department, 26

N

Naylor, Gloria, 24
Nicknames, 7, 74, 113-14
Night Court, 50, 51, 94
Nobody's Child, 28, 48, 90
The Nominative Case, 29, 53, 100-01, 150
Non-traditional student, 6, 11, 29, 51, 52, 61, 155
nurturing, the theme of, 116, 117, 119-21, 146

O

Oakton Community College, 59, 74. *See also* two-year col-
        leges
Oates, Joyce Carol, *xviii*, 37, 98-100
Open-door policy, 11, 45
Oral History, 47, 97
Orfield, Gary, 11, 12, 86
Organizing, the theme of, 124. *See also* cooperative actions

P

Paradise, 24
Part-time student, 32, 62, 107, 111, 114
        in fiction, 62, 95, 96
Pelletier, Nancy, 29, 45, 91
"People's College," 33, 36
Plato, 8, 17, 55, 92
Poorly-prepared students, the theme of, 115-116, 125-27
Portland Community College, 59, 74. *See also* two-year
        colleges
"Pottery Will Get You Nowhere," 45

R

Raleigh, Mike, 30
Raney, 47-48, 97
The Rearrangement, 29, 45, 91
Reasonable Doubts, 98
Re-entry women students, 59, 102, 110-17
        definition, 9
        in fiction, 24, 25, 91, 96, 101, 151, 153
        image, 3, 145

men students, 55
punishment for attending college, 39-40
transformation, *xvii*
Return rate of journals, 62, 108
Returning women students. *See* re-entry women students
Reverse transfer students, 60-61, 124
Revolution from Within, 16, 28, 135
Romance at two-year colleges, 52, 80*n*
"Room for Two," 50, 51, 94
"Runaway housewife," 39, 43-46
Russell, Bertrand, *xiv*

S

Sanderson, Jim, 99-100
"Saturday Night Live," 50-51, 150
Schaeffer, Susan Fromberg, 42, 94
Self-esteem, 80-84
"Shiloh," 1-3, 31, 39, 43, 65, 72, 79, 84
Shotgun Saturday Night, 30
Sibling Rivalry, 27
Siefert, Lynn, 25
"The Simpsons," 50
Single-mention list
        definition, 23
        positive examples, 30
"Six Poets in Search of a Lawyer," 26
Slim's Table: Race, Respectability, and Masculinity, 13-14
Smith, L. Glenn, 158
Smith, Lee, 25, 47, 97
Smith, Page, 89-90
Space Station Seventh Grade, 95
Spinelli, Jerry, 95

The Stand, 42, 92-93
Starting Over, 42, 93
Steinem, Gloria, 16, 28, 135
Stereotypes
    African-American men, 14
    faculty in fiction, 32, 90
    students in fiction, 14, 21-22, 32, 37, 38, 49, 61
    on television, 49
    two-year colleges, 4, 147
Sternberg, Alan, 25
Storyteller, 5, 8, 14
Strangled Prose, 27
Stress, 67, 82-83, 85-87
"Stripping," 99-100
Students in two-year colleges
    attitudes towards faculty, 106, 109-10
    demographics, 147
    demographics in fiction, 37
    holding four-year college degrees, 51, 59
    image, 145
    problems, 115, 121-23
Sylvania Campus, Portland Community College, 59, 74.

T

Tannen, Deborah, 137
Television, fiction on, 28, 32, 49
Thelma and Louise, 40
Them, 37, 99-100
"Thirtysomething," 97
Throw Mama from the Train, 52, 97-98
Transfer to four-year colleges, 63, 66-67
Two-year colleges

definition, 10
demographics, 6, 32-33
image, *xvi-xviii*, 3, 13, 23, 28, 29, 31, 40, 40*n*, 74-75
invisibility, 2-3, 15, 35, 149, 153-57
liberation from addiction in fiction, 40-41
retirement age, 55
transition between "junior" and "community," 36

U

Unions, 107-08

V

Victimization, 13, 117-18

W

Wakefield, Dan, 43, 93
Walker, Walter, 24
Willeford, Charles, 27, 44, 100
Wilson, J. J., 41-42
WLT: A Radio Romance, 102-03, 152
Wolfe, Tom, 27, 157-58
The Women of Brewster Place, 24
The Women's Room, 95-96
"The Wonder Years," 43, 45-46, 70
Wong, Jade Snow, 34-36, 92
Working class, *xi*, 29, 32, 93
"Writing About 'The Other'," 142
"Writing from the Darkness," 159
The Writing Life, 125

Y

You Just Don't Understand: Women and Men in Conversation, 137